Finding Love in a Bread Bowl
&
Other East Texas Folk Tales

by
PATSY JOHNSON HALLMAN

STEPHEN F. AUSTIN UNIVERSITY PRESS 2017
NACOGDOCHES, TEXAS

COPYRIGHT 2017 Patsy Hallman
Book Design: Jonathan Grant
Cover Design: Tristan Brewster
Pen and Ink Drawings: Tristan Brewster

All rights reserved. No part of this publication may be reproduced, stored in a retrieval system or transmitted in any form or by any mearns. For example, electronic, photocopy, and recording--without the prior written permission of the publisher. The only exception is brief quotations in printed reviews.

For more information Contact:

STEPHEN F. AUSTIN STATE UNIVERSITY PRESS
404 Aikman Drive, LAN 203
P.O. BOX 13007
NACOGDOCHES, TEXAS 75962
sfapress@sfasu.edu
sfasu.edu/sfapress
936-468-1078

ISBN: 978-1-62288-169-7

TABLE OF CONTENTS

Chapter I Tales from Long Ago
Finding Love in a Bread Bowl / 9
Mouse-Tainted Butter / 11
No Watery Grave / 13
A Boy Finds Love for a Lifetime / 15
A Nacogdoches Lady / 17
The Famous Groucho Marx! / 19

Chapter II Tales from Families
A Big Tree / 23
Kin Folks / 25
Fearing East Texas Storms / 27
Family Love / 30
A Good Father / 32
A Good Mother / 36
Growing Up in an East Texas Community / 39
Tales from Share-Croppers / 47
Give Us This Day Our Daily Bread / 50
Fannie Picket / 52
A Long-ago Grandmother / 57

Chapter III. Religion in our Lives
Building a Church / 61
A Gift from the Heart / 64
History of a Methodist Church / 66
Young Mr. Stewart's Art Work / 70
Circuit Rider / 72
Remembering Bishop Houston / 75
The Rev. Littleton Fowler / 79

Chapter IV. Early Schools
Early Schools in East Texas / 83
Nacogdoches University and its Building / 87
Sam Houston Speaks! / 90
Officers of Reconstruction / 92
Sister Josephine / 94
Student Memories / 96
Dr. Birdwell - First Days at SFASU / 98
Dr. Birdwell and the Flournoys / 100
Professor Campbell / 102
Teacher, Teacher! / 105

Chapter V. Angels Sightings
    An Angel of Color / 111
    Angels Among Us / 113
    A Big Black Umbrella / 115
    An Angel in a White Coat / 117
    Angels in the Jury Box / 120
    A Whole Flock of Angels / 122
    The Tired Mule / 125
    Holy Cats / 127
    A Barbed Wire Fix / 129

Chapter VI: First Folks, Nacogdoches
    Nacogdoches, Celebrating 300 years! / 133
    A Page from a Young Indian Girl's Diary / 135
    A Page from a Young Spanish Girl's Diary / 137
    A Page from a Young Anglo Girl's Diary / 139
    A Page from a Young African-American Girl's Diary / 140
    A Page from a Young Mexican-American Girl's Diary / 141

Chapter VII. The Paschalls
    Old Name, Old Family: The Paschalls / 145
    The Bear at the Spring / 148
    A Civil War Wedding / 152
    Those Peculiar Paschalls / 154
    The Paschall Penny / 160

Chapter VIII: Celebrating Christmas
    Eggnog Branch or "Christmas, 1836" / 165
    A Family Christmas Story / 167
    A Cold Christmas Made Warm / 169
    The Year Santa Claus Came Twice / 170
    Christmas is Coming; Christmas is Coming! / 172
    Christmas Comes to Everyone / 175

About the Author

A Bread Bowl that Started a Family!

Chapter I
Tales from Long Ago

FINDING LOVE IN A BREAD BOWL

Life – how great is the living, loving, and working! Blessings abound.

 Among my treasures is a "bread bowl" given to me by my Grandmother Johnson. She had it from her mother-in-law, Martha DeMoss Johnson, who had been given it by her mother, Nancy Grider DeMoss. It is old, polished until it gleams from many years of use!

 But, then, it has been used for ages. In pioneer days, the man of a beginning family would carve the large oval bread bowl as soon as possible after their living quarters were completed. A bread bowl was simply a staple in those early homes. Most women kept a mound of flour in the bowl, and when it came time to make biscuits for breakfast, or dinner, or supper, she simply pulled the bowl of flour from its storage spot, and began the bread making. Shaping a hole in the center of the mound of flour, she added soda, salt, lard, and buttermilk, mixing it together with her fingers. When she had a dough of the appropriate thickness and amount for the meal, she pinched off pieces for biscuits. After she put the biscuits to cooking, she covered the bread bowl - with the unused flour still in it - and placed it back on a kitchen shelf until it was needed to make bread for the next meal.

On the other hand, a more fastidious homemaker would return the unused flour to the flour bin, cover the bin, then wash the bread bowl – inside and out – drying it carefully and putting it away until it was needed to make the next meal's bread.

Now there was in those early days in our community a young man of marriage age; in fact he may have been a little past the age. Nevertheless he was ready to get a wife, a home, and start a family. He was troubled, however, about who among the several possibilities, would be a good wife. Finally he talked with his mother about his dilemma. He explained that that were two young women in the community whom he liked very much. He could, he said, love either of them. He just couldn't decide!

"Are you sure?" asked his mother.

"Yes!" he replied with certainty. "I just don't know what to do!"

"Let me think about it," responded his mother.

Soon she called to him and he came to her from the garden where he had been working.

"Thomas," she said, "I have decided to make several pans of biscuits and a few loaves of bread for the next church gathering, and I need two more bread bowls to make that much bread. Since you are thinking about these two young women, why don't you saddle your horse and ride over to their houses and borrow their bread bowls. It will help me and it will give you another chance to speak with each of them."

He agreed, and was soon on his way. Later in the day, he returned with the two bread bowls. One was pristine with cleanliness, polished from much washing and careful drying. The other had flecks of dried flour along the edges and flour was caught in a small crack in the bottom of the bowl."

The mother looked at each bowl carefully. Then she asked,

"Are you still sure you will be happy with either young woman?"

"Yes, I am," he replied.

With that assurance, his mother picked up the clean, polished bowl and said, "The girl who owns this bowl is the one to choose!"

And he did just that.

Folks say that they lived happily ever after!

The Infamous Mouse!

MOUSE-TAINTED BUTTER

The general store – just a step above the trading post – was the center of the community.

In the pioneer days, a majority of our ancestors lived on farms in small communities. Usually the general store was the center of the settlement. Almost anything that families could not produce for themselves was available at that store.

One of its special features was especially important to women in farm families. For while money management was the responsibility of the man of the family, if there were any surplus products, such as eggs, butter, and cream, the storekeeper would buy them to resell, and the money he paid for them was considered the wife's money. These dollars usually represented the only money the farm wife had that was her very own. Here is a tale that comes from the sale of such a product.

Mr. Corbet, who owned the general store, was very accommodating - always buying whatever the women brought to him. Now sometime along about the time just before WWI, his business grew considerably, because he was able to buy a car. With it, he could, during the day, buy whatever fresh food the women brought in, then late in the day he would drive to the nearest railroad station, seven miles away, and send the produce by train overnight to the Dallas market. There the fresh farm products were in great demand.

One morning, Mrs. Smith, one of the local women, came early to see Mr. Corbet.

"Welcome," he said, "I see you have something for me!"

"Yes," she replied, "I have a pound of butter."

"Excellent, I can sell all I can get."

"But," she explained, "I don't want to sell it; I just want <u>to trade</u> it for another pound of butter."

Thoroughly perplexed, Mr. Corbet asked, "I don't understand; why would you want to do that."

The woman hesitated, looked around the store, seemingly worried about the group of men gathered around the wood heating stove, and nervously asked, "Could I talk with you confidentially?"

"Certainly," he replied, "step over here behind the counter."

The woman began, "Now Mr. Corbet, you see my butter, it is perfectly good – a full pound – firm and cool, with a good yellow color; BUT….. this morning I churned just like I do every other day; and when the butter came, I gently scooped it off the top of the milk, washed it and molded it into this fine pound of butter. However, Mr. Corbet (and she lowered her voice again) when I poured the buttermilk out of the churn, there was a <u>dead</u> mouse in the bottom of the churn!

"Or course, as you can see, the butter is just fine, it will be good eating, but, knowing about the mouse, I just can't eat it. Of course, anyone who doesn't KNOW about the mouse, will enjoy it just like any other butter. That's the reason I want to make a trade."

"Oh my," thought Mr. Corbet, "What will I do; I don't want to offend this good supplier of fresh produce; but I certainly don't want to sell mouse-tainted butter!"

He thought for a minute and then he said, "Well, let me see what I can do."

With that said, he took the butter and went into his back room. There he kept tools of all sorts and among them were several butter molds. One mold was rectangular – just the kind and shape the woman had used to shape the pound of butter she was seeking to trade. But he also had some other butter molds that were round, instead of rectangular.

Closing the door to the work room, he carefully unwrapped the woman's rectangular pound of butter and gently pressed into one of the round molds. He let it set for a few minutes than pushed it out onto a sheet of butter paper. Carefully carrying it proudly back into the store, he asked, "Mrs. Smith, would this one be all right for you?"

She looked at that round pound of butter and said with delight, "Oh, yes, yes, and thank you so much Mr. Corbet!'

And away she went; little knowing that she carried her own mouse-tainted butter home with her.

Of course the tale eventually got out, but down home, folks say nobody ever mention the incident to Mrs. Smith.

NO WATERY GRAVE

Now I lay me down to sleep.

Most of our families who immigrated to Texas in the early days came via one of three routes. The came from the north through Clarksville and on to Deep East Texas, or they came through the Deep South states in through San Augustine, or perhaps they came via boat to Galveston and thence north to this area.

There was in those early days a family named Pippin who chose to come by boat. They left the Carolinas, sailed around Florida into the Gulf of Mexico and thence to Galveston. It was a long trip. But they had prepared well. The several women in the family had learned from other pioneers what was needed and they packed those essentials in large trunks. They were filled with clothing, linens, kitchenware, seeds for new gardens, dried foods, tools and some medical supplies. The men organized storage of the trunks in the lowest part of the boat and the several families set sail.

Days passed with easy sailing. Then, with just a few days left before they were to reach land, tragedy struck. As one would imagine, there were several children in the three family groups on board and the crew and other travelers soon grew accustomed to their noises. Usually the sounds were happy ones of children at play. However, sensitive mothers began to hear the whimper of an unhappy baby. It was a weak cry that experienced mothers recognized as a potential problem. In fact, the cries were from a new baby, born only a couple of weeks before the voyage began. The women talked together about what could be done for the little one with the weak, pitiful cries. But none of their treatments worked, for as the days passed all their remedies failed and the child died.

How utterly terrible! Not only had they lost their precious baby, but they knew immediately what would happen – there would have to bury it at sea – and, none of the women, especially the mother, could bear that thought. In small, quiet groups they discussed the problem and finally they decided on a plan. First, they would keep the death a secret from the captain and his crew. Each wife swore her husband to secrecy and then the women carried out the next part of their plan. Quietly, while the ships workers were busy elsewhere on board, they repacked all their trunks, leaving just enough room in one of them for the body of their tiny baby.

The little body lay hidden among the sheets and other linens until the ship arrived in Galveston. There they organized themselves into a wagon train to travel north to their destination.

Along the way, they stopped at the first community cemetery that they found and with permission, they held a real service for their baby. One of the men offered a fitting sermon; another led the group in a song and another offered a prayer.

When the service was over, they buried their baby, marking her grave with a large stone. Then they moved on, with sad, but comforted, hearts.

A BOY FINDS LOVE FOR A LIFETIME

I'll love you forever; I'll love you always!
Sheila McGraw

After the Civil War, my husband's ancestors, like thousands of families, moved to Texas from the war-torn deep South. They were able to buy a small farm in a remote area. There they farmed and became respected members of a small, rural community. School for their two children was important for them and they were sorely disappointed to learn that their local school went only to the seventh grade.

Now the Hallman daughter was a very bright little girl and the local teacher encouraged the family to find a way to send her into town for higher education. Of course, the couple was pleased to think of their daughter could become a well-educated woman – one prepared to live an easier life than theirs had been. But how to accommodate the need for more education when the town school was so far away from their farm? What could they do?

They talked to various people, spoke with their pastor, and made the long trip to town to discuss the possibilities there.

There were, of course, a variety of options but none was just right. Of course the father could not leave the crops to take the young girl into town each day, and no one even through of the mother driving the team and being away from home duties. And they certainly thought their child was too young to be left in town to board with strangers. What to do? What to do?

Finally they decided on a daring plan. The father decided he could teach their son, who was only ten years old, to drive the team. Day after day, all summer long, the boy practiced harnessing the horse to the buggy and driving around the community. Then, at some point during the summer the father went into town and found a widow near the school who would keep the horse and buggy in her back yard each day for a small fee.

The son would be enrolled in the fourth grade, and he, as his sister, was excited, and a bit fearful about going into the "town" school. But on the appointed day, they got up early – at least by good daylight and ate a big breakfast. While they ate, the father got the horse and buggy ready and the mother packed their lunch pails. Then they were off – at a pretty good speed – anxious to be on time for their first day.

And alas, they were late. The girl rushed into the building and was taken to her class while the little boy was pointed to the fourth grade room. When he entered the room, the class was already into the math lesson. Every child was at the black board working a problem. The teacher pointed him to an empty seat and said for him to sit and watch until she had time to get him his books and various assignments.

He sat quietly, resting from the rush of the trip and from the fear of doing something wrong on the first day he had the responsibility of driving the horse to town. Slowly he began to give his attention to those around him. The class was full of 10 year boys and girls. He watched as they worked the math problems on the board. The students were all well-behaved and nice looking. But one little girl was especially pretty. She had long blond curly hair and she worked her problem with confidence. The teacher asked the students to return to their desks when they finished their problem and when this pretty girl finished she moved toward her seat and wonder of wonders, it was right beside his. He was thrilled. He wanted to know her name and more about her. It turned out that she was one of the several daughters of the school superintendent.

He could not believe that this pretty girl would be sitting by him all year! It was too good to be true. But it was. He thought she was the prettiest girl he had ever seen. He began to love her that very first day and from that day and forever he never changed his mind about her beauty and his love for her.

As time passed they all graduated from high school and the boy's sister entered college to become a teacher. The boy studied to become an accountant and the pretty girl, though offered several scholarships, chose to marry the man she met first as a seat partner in the fourth grade! In due time a baby boy came into their family and their lives were filled with family and work, church and friends. Strong in their community and faithful to their extended family, they left a fine legacy of loving and living.

A NACOGDOCHES LADY

Let me grow lovely, growing old...
                                        Karle Wilson Baker

Mrs. Garland Roark was one of the first people I met in Nacogdoches. My husband and I, along with our two babies, had moved from Houston in the fall of 1963 – the very week that Kennedy was assassinated!

It was a cold, wet fall in this small East Texas college town and we rented the only house available for our family. As the rains came, and continued, our laundry piled higher and higher in the tubs and baskets. We did have a washing machine, but no dryer, and of course, the wet weather meant that hanging the wash on a clothes line would be of no help. What to do?

Looking in the telephone directory, I discovered a laundry mat just a few blocks away. That day when my husband came home for lunch, I drove him back to his office and kept the car to take all those baskets of wet clothes to be dried.

I found the place, and soon had the baskets and the babies unloaded. With the dryers filed with our wet wash, I settled the children around me to read to them while the clothes tumbled dry.

No sooner had I begun reading, when the door opened and in came a surprising sight - a woman dressed in her Sunday best – suit, heels, hat, and white gloves. She was followed by an African American woman in a white apron carrying a huge basket of items to be washing. This woman made several trips to the car to get additional baskets. Then she began to fill the machines. The lady in the hat and gloves stood by to supervise the amount of washing powder put into each machine as well as to supply the coins that each machine required. With that done, the lady turned and walked to the area where we sat.

She reached out her hand and as I stood, she said, "I don't know you so I know you are a newcomer to Nacogdoches; I'm Mrs. Garland Roark."

I could not believe it. Here I was in a washateria meeting the wife of one of the most famous fiction writers of the time – Garland Roark – "Wake of the Red Witch" – soon to be made into a movie!

When I regained my voice I asked her to sit with us. And she did. She gave me all sorts of helpful information about the town, invited me to her church, and suggested helpers, such as doctors, whom I might need. When my clothes were dried , she asked her maid to help me fold them and then she helped me get laundry and children to my car.

I shall never forget that grand lady and the rare hospitality she showed to a young stranger.

I later learned that she was from the well-respected, and large Burk Family – successful farmers in a nearby village – ten children – all fine community members. And, of course, she was married to a famous author and living right here in this small town.

THE FAMOUS GROUCHO MARX IN NACOGDOCHES!

...laughter is good for the soul.

In the early part of the last century, the Marx Brothers, a singing group, were scheduled to perform at the Nacogdoches Opera House. Locals say that their comedy act was born during that performance. This is what happened: The musical group was made up of the three Marx brothers: Groucho, Harpo, and Gummo, along with a female singer, Janie O'Riley. They sang classical songs interspersed with dramatic readings. Now the audience was less than enthusiastic with the performance - giving only limp applause after each piece was presented.

Suddenly in the midst of the program, someone yelled, "run-away, run-away" and most of the audience jumped up and rushed to the windows to see the commotion in the streets. Some said it was actually only one stray mule, but long time local story teller, Bob Murphy, insisted it was a whole team of mules racing down Main Street. Regardless of the number, the commotion in the street took almost all the Marx's audience. To try to lure them back to their performance, Groucho and his brothers began to tell jokes and heckle the audience. This change suited the the ticketholders; they laughed and applauded with gusto. And with the obvious success of that new format for their program, the Marx comedy act was born – right here in Nacogdoches.

Some years later, the story had become such a favorite one of local story tellers that the mayor, Mr. Frank Hathcock, wrote to Groucho saying he was being made an honorary citizen of Nacogdoches.* Mr. Marx responded with thanks and good humor. When he died in 1977 after 50 years of performances, the Dallas Morning News reported the death of Groucho Marx and mentioned the Nacogdoches episode in his obituary.

Years passed and when the Nacogdoches Opera House closed, its furnishings were spread about into various city buildings. The upright piano that had been played by the now famous Groucho Marx, was given to the Old University Building. Today, docents proudly show the piano to visitors and tell the Marx story.

The letter Mr. Hathcock received in response to his letter naming Groucho an honorary citizen of Nacogdoches:

April 19, 1954

Dear Mr. Hathcock:

Thanks — I am delighted to be made an Honorary Citizen of Nacogdoches. I will always have a warm spot in my heart for this little town in Texas and if I ever get close to it, by God I'll stop in and see you.

Cordially,

Groucho Marx

Chapter II
TALES FROM FAMILIES

"THE BIG TREE"

I think that I shall never see a poem lovely as a tree.
                                                    Kilmer

    A huge post-oak, it stands proudly in the front yard of the "home place." And, according to our forestry friends, it has been there for almost 300 years. Our people first saw this magnificent tree when Great-grandfather Johnson brought his family to Texas at the end of the Civil War. His was one of those farms virtually destroyed by northern soldiers near the end of the war, and the Johnsons, like hundreds of other families, sold their land and resettled in Texas. They chose a thriving rural community in Northeast Texas. Once he had their log house completed, a few extra pieces of furniture made, and the fields planted, he began his regular work as a Circuit-Rider Methodist Preacher. Traveling south from his farm to the very center of the community, he saw the tree, setting a bit back from the trail and centering a piece of prairie land. My, it was handsome! Sometimes he stopped and ate his lunch sitting under the shade of that tree.

Around 1900, the preacher's son, Walter Johnson, married one of the local Paschall girls, and they looked around for a place to buy and build their first home. How delighted they were when they discovered that the farm with the "big tree" was for sale! Soon it was theirs, and they built their house so that the tree sat directly in front of the house. Walter grew cotton in the field west of the tree, and it was convenient to park the cotton wagon under its branches so that the workers could empty their cotton sacks into the wagon. They rested awhile in the cool shade of the tree before they returned to that backbreaking job of picking cotton.

In 1927, Walter's son, Don, married the first grade teacher in the local school and he and his new wife established themselves in the Johnson home so that they could care for the aging and ailing parents. Don and Edna raised their family in the house beside the "big tree." By now the tree was virtually an extension of the living room. People sat in its cool shade all through the summer and children played on the swing that hung from its high branches. When the garden stuff was ready for picking, the family worked in the shade of tree, shelling peas, shucking corn, peeling peaches and doing other chores that were more comfortably done in the cool shade than in the hot house.

As years passed a fourth generation of Johnsons, Don and Edna's children, grew up playing "under the big tree." There was the swing, the crocket set, the toy cars with their roads running around the tree - here were picnics and sitting on the big rock playing dolls.

Don and Edna's grandchildren were the fifth generation to climb high in the branches of the "big tree." They came with their parents to visit and to play in the shade of the great tree first discovered by their great, great grandfather.

Today, yet a sixth generation of the family enjoy the tree, for when the family all "come home," the tree has become the gathering spot. Last year one limb had become so huge that it threatened to pull the tree to the ground. Foresters came and cut off the huge limb and the tree lives on!

KIN FOLKS

...do not swear by your head, for you cannot make one hair white or black. Let what you say be simply 'yes' or 'no.

Matthew 5

It was not long after WWII and at last the automobile industry was up again and running full speed! Many people bought new cars. Among them was our Jonathan.

He was so proud of the car that one week end he came to our community to show it to his father and his uncle – old men, both of whom still lived down on the farm – neither of them drivers. As they admired the car, Jonathan said, "Papa John, I'd like to take you and Uncle Walter on a short trip – maybe a long day trip or even a trip of a couple of days. Where would you like to go?"

"Oh, my," replied his father; I'll have to think about that – don't know if we could get away."

And so the subject was dropped. However, sometime later after a fine mid-day dinner had been enjoyed by all those gathered, the old men went outdoors to sit under the tree and smoke their pipes. As they sat, Old John said to his brother, "Walter, I've been thinking about Jonathan's offer to take us on a trip in his new car. You know we're long wanted to see the man that is our Grandfather's only brother. Remember, he lives up in Oklahoma, just over the Texas-Oklahoma border. There were only the two boys in the family - him – I think his name is Cecil and our Grandfather Dow. I'm told that Cecil settled there in the edge of Oklahoma at the same time our Grandfather came further south into East Texas."

"I've often thought about him," mused Walter. "I always wondered if he lived the life of our Grandfather Dow. It would probably be unusual to find a family with two Circuit Riders, but surely he's a good Methodist, like others in the family."

"Oh, he's bound to be," said Old John, "Way I've always heard it, any brother of our Circuit Rider Grandfather is bound to be a good man. Great Grandmother's boys would not have got away with any kind of rough speech or raucous living. He may not have become a preacher, but I'm confident he's someone we can call family."

"Tell you what, let's asked Jonathan if he'd like to drive us to Oklahoma – we could start by day-break one morning and get there by dinner time - have dinner with him, visit, and then come home in the evening – might be midnight getting back – but it would be a good little trip."

"Would we be back in time to get enough sleep to be up and about our church duties the next day?"

"Oh, of course, of course."

After more discussion, the trip was planned and on an early, early Saturday morning, right after day-break they set out in the new car!

And what a fine car it was – comfortable and one that sped along the highway with ease. As they crossed the Oklahoma border and entered the first little town, they suggested that Jonathan let them out near the court house while he parked the car. They were confident that they could get directions from the inevitable group of men gathered there for Saturday morning visiting. Johnathan would go on to park the car while they sought information about the location of the Perry home. They were right about finding a group of locals. They sauntered toward the group and when they were in hearing distance they began to pick up on the topics. Seems as politics were the issue of the morning. There was one man in the group that spoke in a very loud voice, with strong opinions. At one point he shouted, using unrepeatable language about the character of some of his companions. Walter and Old John were amazed to hear such – the man's threats, his cursing, and the vulgar language that he used.

Nevertheless they continued toward the group for it was their only source of help in locating the Perry home. When they got to the fringe of the gathering, Walter tapped a fellow on the shoulder and asked, "Could you possible give us directions to the home of Cecil Perry?"

"Sure," replied the fellow. But he's here this morning – right over there." And to the amazement of Old John and Walter, the man pointed to the loud-mouthed one who was still shouting threats, obscenities, and damnation to those who might disagree with him!"

Old John looked at Walter and with sure and swift understanding between the two, Walter said, "We've seen enough; let's go home!"

And that's what they did – sighting-seeing was one thing but establishing a relationship with a man like they had heard for the last few minutes was beyond the pale! They wanted nothing to do with him, relative or not!

FEARING EAST TEXAS STORMS

...a good father is keeper of the family.

When my father was a young boy, his favorite uncle lived in an adjoining community and the families frequently visited together. Uncle Jeremy called my father his favorite nephew and our grandmother said that Father was always happiest when the families were together.

Uncle Jeremy had a wife and three small children, and one particularly stormy spring there was a series of small tornadoes. The family had no storm cellar, so they worried about what they would do if a storm came their way.

On the third day of such storms their fears were realized as a twister in the sky seemed headed directly toward their house. Now Uncle Jeremy had heard what to do in such situations, and fearing the storm would hit their house, he gathered the family together and rushed them to a deep ditch that bordered their property. There the mother, with baby in arms, sat low in the ditch and the other two children sat on each side of her. Uncle Jeremy sort of hoovered over them with arms outstretched to hold them in place as the winds blew fiercely.

And, as feared, the center of the twister hit their barn. The building virtually exploded at the hit. Wood flew in every direction and the barn door flew into the sky, then fell right on top of the family. Uncle Jeremy was killed instantly by the hit, but the positioning of his body saved the rest of the family.

Of course such a tragedy touched the whole community. And my father was so devastated by the death that he vowed this would never happen to his family. He would learn about storm cellars and have one for his own family.

Soon after he married, he did build a cellar for the family; he studied cloud patterns; and he watched them with a vengeance during the storm season that was common to East Texas spring-time.

The cellar he dug was a deep hole in the ground, about 8 x 10 feet, with the whole thing lined with long, thick timbers. Even longer timbers formed the sloping roof. On top of all this was the soil dug from the hole. Four or five steps led down into the place. Benches ran along two sides and shelving for canned foods and fresh fruits was on a third side. The cellar was furnished with blankets; an oil lamp with matches and oil, and a crowbar in case the door was hit – thus wedging the exit.

For our mother the cellar was an excellent place for storing the many foods she canned – corn, tomatoes, chicken stew, hominy, pepper relish, preserves, and other items. In addition, in the fall she bought a bushel of apples and one of pears to preserve for the winter. She wrapped each piece of the fruit in newspaper and returned it to the basket, placing it in a corner of the cellar. In this way we had fruit for the winter.

For my young brothers the cellar provided the very best launching point for bicycles, small cars, and trucks. It was just right, too, for forts that fit into children's play.

Mother would sometimes get impatient with Father's call to go to the cellar if she felt he was over-anxious about a particular storm. But she always went. When he made the call to go, our grandmother grabbed a blanket and, draping her head and shoulders, and rushed to get to her straight chair that was reserved for her in one corner of the cellar. She did make a furtive stop by her bed as she left the house. She was getting her money from the place where she kept it - between mattress and springs! She thought we knew nothing about her cache of funds so we never mentioned it to her. Once, I remember after the storm was over and we were back in the house, my father said to Mother, "Oh my, after you all came to the house, I walked along Mama's path and at my feet just outside the door were three 100 dollar bills. I don't know how many she had, but I at least recovered these for her."

Mother, of course, asked once more, "You can't persuade her to put her money in the bank?"

Father's reply was always the same, "She remembers too well the closing of the banks in her time. I'll just try to be more careful about helping her keep up with it."

For us children, the coming of a storm was a happy time because we knew our friends, the Hatcher family, would come to join us in our cellar. Like Father, Mrs. Hatcher had a great fear of tornadoes, and they had no cellar – so, they came whenever the clouds looked threatening. There were children our age in the family and we had great fun together. Sometimes, after the storm seemed to pass over our area, we would all go into our house waiting lest another twister was sited. In those cases, the

Hatchers would go with us and everyone sat around the fireplace visiting together. Our greatest delight was when we could persuade Mr. Hatcher to tell us a story.

The one he told best was a ghost story from his home in Jeffereson, Texas. It was the tale of "Diamond Bessie." Bessie was a beautiful young woman who had several male friends and each of them had showered her with diamonds, especially diamond rings. No one in Jefferson had ever seen a woman with so many. One day Bessie went missing, and all the men in the town went out in search of her. Eventually she was found, dead, of course, with each of her fingers cut off! Bessie was gone – and so were all her diamonds!

He told other stories that were just as fascinating and we could enjoy them without fears as we sat together in the company of our mothers and fathers in front of the warm fireplace.

FAMILY LOVE

...love is the strongest force in the world...

There once was a young woman, beautiful, smart, and energetic, but very troubled by life events. Despite the fact that she had served as a prosecuting attorney in one of our largest cities, that she had recently won an award for her work with the peace offices of the county, she sat in a psychiatric ward of one of the state's finest hospitals, unresponsive to treatment.

Her mother and father temporarily closed their home and moved to the city to be near her as they and the doctors sought treatment to bring her through a horrible psychosis. "How can we help; how can we help?" Asked the aunts and uncles, the brothers, the cousins, the pastors, and the close friends.

Frustration reigned as help was sought from more and more professionals. Family concern mounted not only for this sick young lady but also for her parents. High blood pressure, heart attacks and stroke are threats that came to mind.

In the midst of this troubled time, an older lady, a beloved cousin of the father, found a way to show her love in an almost angelic manner. She is a woman who grew up in the country with a large vegetable garden, and she continues to make a large garden each year. Once she decided how she could respond the family's tragedy, she set to work. For an entire week, she raided her vegetable garden, picking and shelled, chopped, and preserving the produce. Not one to do anything by halves, she left nothing behind in the garden as she completed her project. When she was finished, she packed her car with the products of her work and traveled to the closed home of the parents of the girl. Knowing the father would check in periodically, she left this message on his kitchen table.

"*Through the years I have had many troubles and you have always helped me through them, supported me, and stood by me. Now it's my turn to help you. I have asked myself over and over: what can I do? I am too old to travel the long road to San*

Antonio; you don't need any money I may have; and I certainly don't have any cures for the sick. But a few days ago, as I gathered vegetables from my garden, I remembered how much you enjoy the foods of our childhood, when we all lived in the country, and I decided on something I could do. GO LOOK IN YOUR DEEP FREEZE."

Love,
Your favorite cousin

A few days later, when the doctors gave a more positive report of the young woman's healing, the father drove back home to check on the place, and, of course, he found the note. Going into his utility room, he opened the door of the freezer, and was startled to see overflowing shelves! Shelled peas, corn-on-the-cob, okra, salsa, butterbeans, squash – dozens and dozens of packages of freshly prepared food from the garden.

As he stood there in front of that open door with the cold air from the freezer rushing onto his face, he cried the tears of the comforted, amazed at the power of family love and thankful for the compassion of angels in aprons.

(With love and fine medical care the young woman was soon restored to health and is, once again, a happy, productive young professional.)

A GOOD FATHER

He knows all about them and loves them just the same.

The father was the third son of Walter and Lola Johnson, thin, like the Johnson men, and dark, like his French grandmother DeMoss. When his mother was asked why everyone called him Don, when his name was Clabern Green. She replied, "I don't know, but when the school officer came to our house to enroll him for first grade, he heard me give his name and he said, 'No, no, put down that my name is Don!'" He was so adamant about it, that she agreed, and he was ever after known by that name.

He completed the education available to him in the local grammar school and used his keen mind to make a good life for his family – first choosing a fine mate – the tall, pretty first-grade teacher. Because he was the last child to marry, he felt it was his responsibility to take care of his parents, so when he married, they simply moved into the family home. They often wished for a home of their own, but they never voiced dissatisfaction at what he considered his lot in life – to care for the aging parents.

His daughter spoke of an early memory.

"There was to be an ice cream social at Miss Annie's house – just a block away from our home. But, because the Mother was pregnant, she could not go, so Father took me - a 3-year old. I rode on his shoulders down the dirt room to Miss Annie's. There the women entertained me on the porch while Father visited with the menfolk. Then Miss Annie filled a syrup bucket with ice cream for Mother, and Father and I raced home to get it to her before it melted!"

Besides the mother and children, the father loved two people most in the world. They were his father and his double first cousin, Sebren Johnson. The two families visited often, taking turns going to each's place. After a brief visit of the whole family, the two men would go away by themselves; sit under the big tree, inspect the garden, look at their newest cattle, or just walk together and talk. They seemed to have a physic bond.

For example, occasionally of a Sunday morning, the father would say, "I expect Sebe and them to come today!" And odd thought it may seem, they usually did arrive before lunch time.

The father never seemed to stop grieving for the loss of his own father. Once, late in life, he went to a family funeral some distance away. There he saw an uncle who looked a lot like his grandfather; he described the experience for us children. He said, "I looked at Uncle Merit sitting near the window of the church and it was like seeing Pappy all over again! How I wish it really had been him!"

The father was a strong family man, loving the mother and working always to take care of his family. Once when she was hospitalized, he would not sleep in their bedroom. He said he was waiting for her to come home to sleep again in their bed.

He was always proud of his children; supporting them in every way he could. Son Lynn told this story. "When I was a teenager, some prowler took some items from the school gym and several of us boys, who had been practicing basketball in the gym, were called in by the superintendent for questioning. When I got home from school, I told our parents about the incident, and immediately our father went to the school and said in no uncertain terms to the superintendent, "my sons are honest, and they would never take anything that was not theirs, nor would they ever cause any trouble. I don't want to ever hear of you questioning the integrity of either of them again!" Lynn said that ended the matter and he was never treated with less than respect from that day forward!

The father was proud of each of his – two for their Ph.Ds. and work as university professors, but it was his young lawyer's work that seemed to give him most pleasure. Occasionally he went into town to hear him in court, and he always came away greatly pleased.

Once when the oldest boy was in law school, he wrote home about a difficult class he was taking – said he did not know if he could get a passing grade in it. The mother read the letter to the father who said, "You write back and tell him he doesn't have to stay there if he doesn't want to; he can come home and go into business with me!" (Actually, I think the mother wrote back and said, "You can do it!" and he did pass the courses and the bar exam on the first try, to become the fine, successful lawyer he has always been.)

A daughter said, "One of my most cherished memories of Daddy's decision making and influence on my life came was when I was about 10 years old. The Hatcher family had moved to our community to teach and with three children and a family love for music, Mrs. Hatcher arranged for a music teacher to come from the nearest town to give piano lessons. Of course, to make that happen she had to get several parents to agree to pay enough to make it worthwhile for the teacher to drive the distance to our community once each week. Now, at the time, I was in Mrs. Hatcher's room, and one day in her efforts to find students, she said, "You have finished your work for the morning. Why don't you go home and ask your father if you can take lessons?" I jumped up with excitement and raced toward home.

As I ran passed the store porch, there sat Daddy with several other men. I stopped and asked, "Daddy, may I take piano lessons if Mrs. Hatcher gets a teacher to come; it will cost fifty cents a lesson." He immediately replied, "Sure, if that's what you want to do!" I raced back and began what has been a major joy in my life – the piano."

He was an old-fashioned man with regard to women and children. I don't know what his language among the men might have been, but in the company of the family the strongest thing he said when he was aggravated was, "Well, I'll be dad-blamed!"

He made a living first as a farmer, working the family land and 40 acres that he and Mother bought, but also doing extra work for others when his crop was "laid-by" and during the winter. Once during the Great Depression, someone at the store said that a man looking for someone to paint the outside of his house. The father immediately said, "I think I can do that." And he did, earning in a couple of days that were required to do the job a healthy sum of $4.00.

That experience led him to begin a paint contracting business that he worked at until retirement. He taught his sons the trade and each of them worked their way through undergraduate degrees painting houses in a local university town. He continued farming for many years, but soon after WWII ended, cotton farming moved to west Texas and the father, like all his neighbors found other work.

He was a strong church man, in services every Sunday, on every church work-crew, and always alert to see that the church had a good preacher.

He often drove the 20 miles into town to do errands on Saturday mornings. Occasionally he would take one of the children with him. Once, during WWII, he came home with a pair of silk stockings for his wife. She was aghast to see them. "How," she wondered, "could he have found them in war time, AND how much had he paid for the?" She wore them proudly for a long time, careful to mend them when there was a runner.

He was a generous man, always a part of the group of men who "made up" for some family who might need help. He would come home from the country store and say to his wife, "The men at the store are making up for the Jones; I put in a few dollars; can you get some canned food to put in the box?" And, of course, she did. He particularly loved sharing the vegetables he grew in his huge garden.

His children never doubted his love and care for them.

A GOOD MOTHER

...when your community asks you to do something, you do it!

When Joe and Edith Smith saw their baby girl, Mary Edna, she was immediately special to them. They already had a boy and their first baby girl had died, so they were very proud to get little Edna. Edith solicited her maiden sister, Mame, to help make her first best baby dress. By the time they had it made, she was about one year old, and with a matching bonnet and her first hard-soled shoes, she was a beauty. They had a photographer come and take her picture of her in her finery!

During all her life, Edith depended on Edna. In just a few years, she became a great help in care of the house, as well as in the field. As an adult, Edna visited her mother every two weeks, and on the visit there was always work to be done – sewing, canning, or working at some other family task.

In school, our mother was a model student, well-behaved and one who excelled in all her classes. She loved to learn, and she was a life-long learner. Once when she was admonishing us children to do our very best in school, she said we might not always achieve perfection, but, if we did our best, we could be satisfied with our efforts. Then she illustrated with one of her experiences. It happened when she was in college taking an advanced literature class. Despite her best efforts, she went home at the end of the term, thinking she had failed the course. When the mail brought her grade report, she discovered that she had not failed; rather she had made a D! "I was happier about that grade than any one I ever made," she exclaimed.

Work in the Smith family was never ending. Edna once described a day at home in her years as a growing child and young woman. "Each morning while Mama was dressing she called me to get up. Soon I was in the kitchen to take over the breakfast preparations while Mama went to the barn to help with the milking. After breakfast Mama and I washed the dishes, then we went to school or on weekends, summers and holidays, we went straight to the fields. There was always work to be done on a truck farm! When we came home from school we were hungry and Mama always had something for us to eat – it was often a warm sweet potato that had slowly cooked all afternoon in the oven of the wood cook stove. We got one and went out on the back porch steps and sat and ate it while it was warm, sweet, and waxy. Delicious! Soon it was time to help Mama start supper and again as she went to milk the cows, I finished getting supper on the table. With only lamps for light we went to bed early."

Fanny Pickett, Edna's grandmother who lived just across the road, up a bit, but in sight of their house, was a great mentor for Edna. She shared good books with her, taught her to play the piano, gave her a love for gardening, and taught her to sew.

Mother was an excellent seamstress making new clothes for us and, at times, cutting down clothes in order to make them fit me. I remember when her brother went to WWII he gave her several of his work suits. She ingeniously cut and sewed them into coat suits for herself! We thought she looked so smart in her new wardrobe!

She loved teaching school – was the primary teacher in Miller Grove from the time she was 17 years old until she was 26. After her first child was born, she served as the substitute teacher, but she never again accepted a full year contract.

In 1955, she worked for a year or so in Greenville at the Henson Garment Factory and still later she worked in Sulphur Springs at Cannon Craft for several years. She enjoyed commuting with several Miller Grove friends and she enjoyed her work as a programmer in the Cannon Craft Office.

She was a great community person. I remember a mother who was always working in whatever group she was involved at any given time. For example, at the church, she played the piano, taught Sunday school, helped organize the Bible Schools, and was on every work team that organized to care for the building. On Sunday's she often served dinner to the preacher.

The same pattern emerged with regard to the school: she attended every parent function, sewed costumes for the programs, served as PTA president more than once, and in general supported the whole system. Not the least of this support was seeing that all three of us were active in as many school activities as were appropriate for us.

In the community at large, she helped care for the sick, served food to families of the dying, and encouraged and helped anyone whose need crossed her path. She was a beloved friend of the whole community – many of whom had been her students when they were children.

She was retired for only one year before her death, but in that year, she visited each of her children for several days each. She recovered a sofa, refinished her bedroom suit, sewing some clothes, and completed 19 oil paintings. We are proud to have them hanging in our various homes and in the homes of our children.

As we grew up, we always knew Mother had the kind of love that is never divided, but rather is multiplied. We never, ever, doubted her love for us and for our father. We also knew our mother was a wise woman, quietly and tactfully giving us advice when she felt us, as adults, needed it. Mother and Daddy set high goals for us and helped us to reach them. We owe them much for our good lives.

Words fail me to describe the good Mother that she was and the fine person that she was. We like to say, "Everyone thinks their mother was perfect, but ours really was!"

The book, LETTERS FROM MISS EDNA, gives a much clearer picture of this wonderful woman, community member, teacher, daughter, wife, daughter-in-law, worker, and mother.

GROWING UP IN A EAST TEXAS COMMUNITY

...home is where the heart is!

Older folks (eighty-ish) among us, tell of growing up in another world – the world of World War II and its aftermath. They speak of family, of schools, of economics, and the work world.

Our Family

My first memories of home were of our family of five: Mother, Father, our Grandmother Johnson, our Grandfather Johnson, and me. However, we were seldom just five, for one or more relatives or neighbors came by every day, perhaps Aunt Virgie with her three children, or Uncle Walter, or Auntie Faye. Moreover, our Grandmother Johnson had, at various times, four sisters within the community, each with large families. Their children, too, were frequent visitors, coming at most any time of the day because, as was common in the time, women with children did not work outside the home, giving them freedom to visit or work together on various projects at any time of the day and evening. I was four years old before Coy was born, and that was the year that our grandfather died, making us still a family of five until Lynn was born when I was eleven years old. It was only six years later that I went away to college.

The House

We all lived in the house that our grandparents had built in 1910. It included a front porch (where the family sat after supper in spring, summer, and fall), and a "front room" which we often referred to as "the house." For example, if we were in the kitchen after supper, I might say something like, "Mama, I'll help Mother finish the dishes; you go on into the house." I suppose this was an old phrase used since the days when kitchens were not a part of the main house. In addition, there was the "middle room," the kitchen, and the back porch. The latter was centered with the cistern, making it very convenient to get water whenever it was needed. This back porch had a "wash shelf" with soap, hand towel, and water bucket by the back door. There was a large closet in the corner of the porch which was used for storage of linens and work clothes. It was also the location for the washtub where we took our "tub" baths, though at times we just took a wash pan of hot water with soap and cloth to our bedrooms for bathing. And finally there was "our room" where Mother, Daddy, Coy and I slept in two double beds when we children were small. However, before Lynn was born, the house was remodeled to make a kitchen of the back porch, giving us more bedroom.

Built in 1910 by our grandparents, ours was always a tidy, clean house, and our father always kept it painted. Once when a group of girls were talking together, the topic of financial status came up. One of them said, "Of course we don't have as much at our house as some of you have." One replied, in an effort to make her feel better, "well, we don't have any more than others." To which she said, "But your house is painted!"

To describe our house without mentioning the "big tree" is a mistake, for, all times of the year, weather permitting, it served as an extended living room. Children played under it; men gathered there to talk after Sunday dinner; and women worked in its shade to shell peas, shuck corn, and do all manner of outside work on hot days. When we were children there was a fine swing in the tree and as we played together someone was usually swinging high into the branches of the tree. After we were gone from home, Father put the porch swing on a tree limb and that was his favorite place to relax.

Our place had 25 acres, half surrounding the house and half across the road. The garden, smokehouse, woodpile, and toilet were important components of the "house" side of the property and across the road were the barn, chicken house, and pig pen, spaces for parking the cultivator and other farm machinery, and the stock pool. When our grandparents bought the place in the early 1900s there was a log cabin on the southeast corner of the farm where the family lived until they built around 1910.

The Community

From the front door and the windows in the front room, a view of the whole community was readily available to us. A glance would tell us whose car was at the store, which had already driven into the church parking lot, and whether or not the buses had arrived at the school. This was true because our house was in the very center of the community. The Methodist Church was across the road in front of the house, and the school and store were in the other two corners of the community's intersection.

Of course, ours is the "third" center of the Miller Grove community.

First, in the early days of the settlement of the community, the trading post was the center. By the Civil War time, the center had been moved to the area near a large lake. Then in 1941, when the road that connected our community to the nearest town, was paved, the stores and post office all moved near the schools and churches which were already in the vicinity of our house. I remember seeing the movers slowly inch one of the stores along the road to its new location. The storekeeper never closed during the move; customers just hopped up into the store as it rolled along if they wanted to buy something. Only the blacksmith and gin pool were left to mark the place of the old businesses. Our grandfather sold a lot from his pasture to the store owner so that the business could be located in the center of the community.

Since it was built in 1899, the Methodist Church has always been on its present location, however, it originally faced the west. With the road paved, it was turned to face the east. Our parents remembered the controversy that erupted over turning the church.

At that time, there was only one other church in the community. It was the Presbyterian Church, located on a lot our grandfather let them use that was behind the general store. The stores, the school, a sawmill, and the two churches completed the public areas in our community.

Communication

We had several means of keeping up with everything going on in the community. There was, of course, the visual sense of people's movements, but there was also the telephone system with several families on the same line. When the phone rang, anyone on the line could pick up the telephone receiver and listen to the conversation. Mother discouraged this ill-mannered practice, but if Grandmother Johnson were home alone and bored, she was not beyond catching a bit of news in that way. Our own telephone ring was one long and two shorts and we were not meant to pick up unless our ring sounded. There was also the "line ring;" it was seven longs, and when it sounded, someone in every family on the whole telephone system rushed to hear the emergency message. It was usually something like, "fire at the Corbet – all hands needed," or maybe something like "there is to be a line-working on Saturday; we need all men to meet at Ed's store and divide into teams to repair the lines – the line to Cumby is completed down."

Other means of communication included the news our father brought home daily from the store porch. He brought all the information and shared it with us, or, if it were not appropriate for all to hear, he waited until they went to bed, where he and Mother talked quietly about the day's events.

We did get the weekly Hopkins County newspaper, and we always had a radio that was set for news at six in the morning and six in the evening. During WWII, I was a child, and I hated having to hear Grabrial Heater give those six p.m. war reports. Eventually, I realized I could leave the room and avoid hearing his booming voice tell of the many battles and the plight of the poor Jews who were being sent to gas ovens.

In those days, Mother wrote often to her family, usually on Sunday afternoons, but the main communication via the mail was with postcards. Our grandmother kept in touch with her son who lived in Dallas with cards and our Grandmother Smith often sent cards to Mother. They were called "penny postcards" because a penny would mail them.

Home Work

Our days began early with our father rising first and, in winter time, starting a fire in the fireplace and in the cook stove, before he went to the barn to milk, feed, etc. In early days, that included carry the kitchen waste to the pigs on his way to the barn. Or perhaps my brother carried that in his little red wagon as one of his morning chores. Mother and Grandmother Johnson were soon up cooking breakfast and we children were called in time to dress and eat breakfast with the adults. Each of us had tasks; as soon as he was big enough my brother helped at the barn, and I made beds and swept the living room before we went to school. We rushed about to get there on time, but we could hear the first bell from our house so we could always get there before the tardy bell rang even if we were running later than usual.

After breakfast, Mother packed Father's lunch – perhaps a boiled egg, ham or sausage on biscuits or "light" bread, a fried pie, and whatever else was left over to add to his menu. Nevertheless, our main meal was always at noon and we children came home from school to eat. Supper was left-overs from noon with perhaps a hot dish or two added – maybe fried potatoes and hot biscuits or fried ham and gravy.

We always went to church and Sunday school on Sunday; likewise our family was as faithful to every school event – basketball games, plays and other programs. The boys played basketball, but my lackluster attempts at sports extended only to an occasional member of a girls' baseball team. I usually took my piano lessons during the P. E. period, or just stayed in study hall and read.

In summers we shared whatever work there was to do – early in our lives that was picking cotton in the fall, but later it was giving music lessons for me and helping our father for the boys. For cotton picking, our work lives were greatly improved when the cotton gins were adapted to allow for processing the whole cotton burr rather than just the fuffy inner cotton fibers. After that change, we "pulled" cotton, meaning we took off the entire ball, thus being able to work without as much injury to our hands. We could also make more money by pulling rather than picking. I remember getting $3 a hundred pounds for picking and $2 a hundred for pulling. By the time I was eleven or twelve years old, I could usually pull four hundred pounds a day, thus making $8. In a season of about 4 or 5 weeks, I could make enough money for my personal spending for the year. There was also a little left over each time for my "college savings account." Mother wrote in my brother's memory book that he pulled 250 pounds one day when he was nine years old. That earned $5.00 for him!

As children, summers held special chores as well. We helped with "cleaning" the yard – a chore we detested even if it were only hauling off leaves in our red wagon. We also had to help with picking and canning food from the garden. Picking and canning (or freezing) corn was the biggest workday. Father and the boys picked great loads of it and carried it to the workplace under the big tree. There we shucked it, brushed away the silks, washed it in big tubs, and cut it off the cobs into great pans. Mother usually manned the heating of it in the hot kitchen and placed it either in jars for canning or bags for freezing. This massive production of food for the winter (for all our kitchens as we grew up and had places of our own) was a great source of satisfaction for our father.

The School

Mother was the first and second grade teacher in Miller Grove for eight years, but she gave up the position when I was born. (Our status in the community was always a cut above average because we were "Miss Edna's" children.) Miss Lennon was the first teacher for all three of us and we loved her. She had had teacher training from SMU and brought the very latest methods home to Miller Grove. For example, her room had weather chart and each day someone was responsible for assessing the weather and posting it first thing in the morning. There was a sandbox where we built hills and mountains, roads and the towns, and all sorts of geographic formations. We learned to read from the "Big Book." The sight reading method was considered the best way to learn reading in her day. We learned about Dick and Jane and Spot and were soon reading from more advanced texts. She guided each of us in plays for parents at Thanksgiving and in each year's great May Day Festival. Once when my little brother, Lynn, and our cousin,

Ginger, both four years old, were to be crown bearers for the crowning of the Queen of May, we lost the two little fellows. When Mother and Aunt Faye looked around and could not find them, they sounded the alarm. There were people everywhere, so it was not easy to search. The gym was packed with parents and performers were lined up in the school hallway. It was almost time for me to play the piano procession. But everything stopped and various ones began looking in every nook and crannie. Mr. Robinson, the high school English teacher, .rushed out to the school well and jerked up the lid to see if by some chance they had fallen in! In desperation Mother went into the gym to create search teams for the grounds and surrounding area when she spotted the two little formally-clad performers. They were standing in the corner of the gym right where someone had told them to wait. The day was saved! And the show went on!

Miss Lennon gave each of us a good start – a foundation that a few years later allowed us to graduate in the honors category. Miss Lennon grouped me with a smart little girl named Mary Frances Johnson, my second cousin, and we completed first and second grade work in one year, then the next year we were moved to Mrs. Junell's room for third, fourth, and fifth grades.

I loved books and I shall never forget one of my great discoveries in Mrs. Junell's room. It happened one day during our study time. I had finished my work and as I looked across the aisle at a fourth grader I saw that she was reading a book that was not the textbook. I asked where she got it. "Oh," she replied, "there's a whole bookshelf on the fifth grade side of the room and you can get one and read it whenever you finish your assignments." I could not believe such a luxury! I went immediately over and selected a book called, "Uncle Wiggle Goes to Town." From that early discovery, reading for pleasure has been a delightful part of my life!

In our high school, the curriculum was set; everyone took the same courses. Electives were Ag and home economics and everyone "elected" them. Our only science was a general science course. I remember being told in college that I must take two chemistry courses; I had no notion of what that subject matter would be. Fortunately, with kind and helpful teachers, I soon learned and escaped with B's in both courses. We three graduated from high school with honors and did fairly well in college, and now we are in the midst of good and satisfying living. Many others from Miller Grove have done equally well or better. In our time that little rural consolidated school has produced doctors, lawyers, school administrators, teachers, military men, good farmers, and at least couple of millionaires!

Probably we owe much of our success at school to our mother. Every evening she supervised our homework, and she was always a part of the school community. We profited from her work and her reputation as an educator. For example, we always had excellent parts in performances and opportunities for enriching activities. Someone asked me not long ago, if I am nervous before speaking engagements. I replied that I am seldom bothered by speaking to a group, because our mother had us children up before groups from the times of our earliest memories. (Our mother was a product of a long line of strong women – one of special significance for her, and through her, for us, was mother's Grandmother Smith. That lady taught my mother to love books, to play the piano, to do fine needle work, to appreciate and grow beautiful flowers, to be activity in the community, and to grow up knowing that she would go beyond her small rural school to experience higher education.)

Big Events in Our Young Lives

Ours were busy lives, for our parents participated in every community event whether it was the summer revival at the church (usually one or two weeks), school sporting events, plays, or socials such as community ice cream suppers. Mother was several times the PTA president and Daddy was a church leader and for a time, a school trustee. In my memory, here are some things that I remember with great pleasure:

- High school plays, programs, banquets, Christmas programs, piano recitals, etc. (For my brothers, these included ball games and tournaments). For example, on the last day of school each year we had a big community "stew," and that was extra special. All our parents came – mothers brought ingredients for the stew and fathers made it in big iron pots that sat on hot wood fires built in the yard behind the school building.
- I remember it was at school on a hot summer day in 1945 when we heard the news that the war was finally over. Chat Corbet had rigged up a wire to a portable radio and set it on a table under a tree so that our parents could listen to the exciting news as they peeled and canned pineapples for the school's lunch program (surplus foods given to the school by the government.) We children played about, eating the pineapple left on the "core" of the fruit; juice dripped down our chins and our arms; it was delicious!

- Visiting the relatives – usually Grandmother Smith or Mother's brothers and sisters. Or perhaps, Uncle Sebe and Aunt Dove (Daddy's favorite relatives)
- Going with our friends, the Hatchers, to the County Fair, or to a movie, or to some other event they invited us children to share.
- Having our friends come to play – usually under the big tree. In my time the friends were the Robert Johnson girls (same surname, but not relatives), the Hatcher kids – Wanda, Margaret, and Charles Wesley, and Peggy (our cousin). Often we went home with each other after church, ate with the family then played all afternoon.
- Having adult visitors in our home. Often on Sundays this was the preacher, because some family had to invite him to eat each Sunday as it was too far for him to return home for a meal and of course, there were no restaurants in M. G. Other times it was Daddy's Uncle Bloom and his cousin Sebren and wife, Dovie.
- Christmas with all its special activities. Fruit salad (tossed in our own heavy cream), hot rolls, and all sorts of desserts.
- High school graduation and successful college days that resulted in eight degrees for the three of us with not a thought of a college loan!

Each of us worked to help with our expenses. The boys were contract painters and I was a secretary in an administrative office. Eventually we all earned additional degrees at other universities, giving each of us the doctoral status – two Ph.D.'s and one law degree. Mother was especially proud when each of those was awarded. And each of us has a fine life partner and wonderful children. We hope they are proud of us, for they made our good lives possible. What a great life they gave us – one that continues to be happy and fulfilling for all three of us and our families.

The time of Mother's untimely death from leukemia at only 66 years of age is still too sad to recount. But, as time passed, we were happy that Daddy managed to live as fully as possible to the fine age of 93.

After many years of living elsewhere, and after traveling to countries far and near, our roots still lie in Miller Grove. Perhaps, for us, there is no place of peace any more comforting than gathering with each other and friends and other family members to sit together and visit "under the big tree."

TALES FROM THE LIVES OF SHARE-CROPPERS

...we will find a better place next year...

Toward the end of the 19th century – after the Civil War, the Reformation, and all the upheaval brought about by the north-south conflict, there lived in Deep East Texas a sharecropper named Frank Tatom. Frank and his wife, Theodocia Scott, were much loved by their immediate and the extended family. They led a simple life, never owning their own land, but working always as share-croppers, and living in whatever house the land owner provided for them.

"Share-cropping" was a common form of farming in early America. The owner of a farm hired a man and his family to live on a portion of his property and work the land. When the produce was harvested and sold, the owner and the share-cropper shared the profits, with the land owner taking the larger share. Share-croppers moved often – always looked for a situation that offered better housing and/or better (more productive) farm land. Theodocia and Frank worked as share-croppers all their lives.

Theodocia's father had an interesting and mysterious history. His name was Perry Scott and he was a school teacher in Cumby, Texas, although he had been reared somewhere in the "north." His wife was a southern girl named Mary Ann Fields. One day, not long after the Civil War began, Perry said to Mary Ann, "I must make a trip north to get books for the school. Take care of our babies while I am gone!" That was the last anyone in the family ever heard of Perry Scott.

As the years passed and May Ann aged, she would tell the story, sorrowfully, "He kissed me goodbye, and I watched him go down the road until he was out of sight; I never saw or heard of him again." For years the family speculated about what happened. Some asked, "Could he have sympathized with the cause of the north and left to go and fight for the Federalist?" Others asked, "Was he simply killed along the way as he traveled to buy the books?"

No one in the family was ever able to solve that mystery!

Eventually Mary Ann took her children and moved back to a farm near her mother and step-father. There her half-brothers helped her make a cotton crop. They did the plowing while Many Ann and her daughters, Theodocia and Margaret Derashaugh, did the planting and hoeing and gathering. When Theodocia grew up, she married Frank Tatom and they invited her mother, Mary Ann, to live out her life in their home.

Frank, was a good farmer - much sought after by landowners who wanted families to live on the property and work the land. For that reason, the family moved about every two years – always looking for more productive land or for a better house for the family. For example, during his lifetime, Frank Tatom and his family lived in these East Texas communities: Old Tarrant, Brashear, Pleasant Grove, Liberty, Sherley, Chapman Arms, Birthright, Shady Grove, Alba, Paint Rock, Shooks Chapel, and Tarapins Neck.

The children were always sad when moving day came and they had to leave their friends. But when they got to the new community, their father would say to them, "you go to this new school and church with your heads held high; you are just as good as anyone who is somebody!"

The Tatom children, of course, grew into adults and became fairly successful people. When they got together for a visit they often related stories of their childhood. This was one of their favorites:

We moved one Saturday late in the fall. Of course we didn't know anybody and had nothing to do on Sunday afternoon, so Pa said, 'Let's take a walk in the woods.' Off we went, Ma and the little kids, too. It was a pretty place; we found clear, clean spring water to drink and some hickory nuts to take home for Ma's Christmas Cake. We played on the grapevines, swinging across the creek. Then Pa spotted a possum high in a tree. He was delighted, for he wanted to get that animal for our dinner. He had not brought his gun, so he climbed the tree and captured the possum with his bare hands. When we got home he skinned it and put it on the roof so that the frost would fall on it during the night. The next day Ma roasted it with baked sweet potatoes and it was surely good – all ready for us to eat when we got home from our first day in the new school.

The family spent their evenings sitting around the fireplace or, on warm days, on the front porch. There they sang together and often told ghost stories. Here is their most mysterious goast story:

"One of our family moves was from Brashear to Liberty, and with that lengthy distance it was necessary for us to spend one night on the road. As it began to get dark, Pa stopped the wagon at a farmhouse and asked if they could take us in for the night. The farmer said, 'No' he had no room, but that there was a vacant house just down the road. 'I must warn you though,' said the farmer, 'folks around here say the house is haunted.'

'Well,' replied Pa, 'I ain't afraid of haints!' and he preceded to drive to the place and

get us settled in for the night. He made pallets on the floor of the front room close enough to the fireplace to stay warm and we were soon asleep.

Now on the outside chance that there were ghosts about, Ma and Pa decided to leave a lamp burning all night. After Ma had got all the babies asleep and the older children settled into their blankets, she was about to pull up her own covers when she glanced at the lamp and saw THREE FINGERS REACH DOWN INTO THE LAMP'S CHIMNEY AND EXTINUISH THE LIGHT! She hurriedly relighted in but the same three fingers put out the light again! With that, she waked Frank and told him what she had seen. He got up and loaded his gun and sat guarding his family for the remainder of the night. The lamp light did not go out again, but the family made haste to leave the place at first light'!"

"GIVE US THIS DAY OUR DAILY BREAD"

(and meat, fruit, and vegetables, too, please)

Prior to World War II, a majority of the population of the United States lived in rural areas where they farmed for a living. This changed, of course, after the war, but many of those small family farms continued in one form or another for several years. Life in the country included a way of life foreign to today's young adults and for many middle aged people as well. In fact, today it takes a senior citizen to explain how the majority of people lived. Terms that were common then are virtually foreign today. Expressions like hog-killing, canning, doing up the night work, etc., take some explaining. Perhaps our food habits have changed as much as anything. Consider, for example, how a farm family produced its own food.

Gardening

Menus were dictated by foods available in family gardens. These were planted beginning in February – in fact, in Nacogdoches, if a farmer did not have his corn planted by Valentine's Day, he was considered a foolish fellow! East Texans could expect meals in the spring to reflect what was ripe in the vegetable garden and that included new potatoes, English peas, green beans, squash, cabbage, onions and radishes. Those items served along with hot cornbread made a meal for noon and evening (dinner and supper). Later there came corn, field peas, okra, and tomatoes. During the winter months, there were the garden foods which the homemaker had canned or dried. Of course every meal included hot biscuits!

Meats

Some families had meat every day but many had meat only for company or on Sundays. The meat was usually fried chicken, chicken pie, or chicken and dumplings. Of course, after "hog-killing" there was smoked ham, shoulder meat and middling meat. This pork was important to a well-fed family. Its preparation began deep in winter time – at the first good freeze. On a cold morning, with a hard freeze, the farmer would get up early and call to the whole family: "Get up and get dressed as soon as you can – we'll kill hogs today." Usually he had a friend with whom he traded work for the butchering, and if so, he would add to his wife, "Call ….. and see if he can come help." Everyone had work to do after a quick breakfast. Outdoors, the farmer built a fire around a big wash pot which he filled by drawing water from the cistern. As the water heated, he checked the butcher knives to be sure they were freshly sharpened, then he went to the pig pin and killed a couple of full grown hogs. These he pulled onto a sled which was then pulled by a horse to the area of the wash pot. Soon the water was boiling and it was poured into a barrel. With one or two others who came to help, the hog heads were sliced off and then each hog was dipped into the hot water. This loosened the hairs, and the work of "scrapping" began. When it was clean, they strung the carcass on a nearby tree limb and set to work butchering it into pieces. There were ribs, back-strap, shoulders, middlings, hogs feet, and the most important parts – the hams. As they cut, they sliced off the fat tissue and tossed it into another iron pot which was waiting in the fire to be used for "rendering" the lard – that is, converting the fat tissue into lard for cooking all year. (The taste of lard was not mild enough for baked desserts – butter was used for them - but the lard was needed all year for frying foods. It was stored in syrup buckets and was considered to be an essential to a well-stocked kitchen.

While the men were scrapping and cutting the meat into parts, the women were also busy. One was called upon to stir the fat meat cooking on the outdoor fire so that the cracklings would not burn; another was grinding the odd parts of meat snipped off the major parts and thrown into a large container to be ground into sausage. Another was cleaning the hogs head – scraping it, removing the eyes, throwing that waste away. With the head nicely cleaned she put it in a large pot for boiling. When it was tender, she deboned the whole thing using the meat for two things. First, she made most of it into souse for sandwiches, but secondly she saved a quart or two of it for making mincemeat. (Later she would add dried fruits, canned fruits, ribbon cane syrup and spices to it and have it available all winter for wonderful "mincemeat" pies!)

With the butchering finished, the farmer sat a low fire in the smokehouse and there the hams, shoulders, and middlings were smoked for preservation throughout the winter. (Later they used an easier method and one that resulted in a better, milder taste. This method was called "sugar curing" the meat.)

At the day's end, the helpers were given a generous share of the meat and the farmer's wife made a delicious evening meal with fried back strap, brown gravy, and hot biscuits.

FANNIE PICKETT

...our lives, our works, our deeds, will continue in others..

Rosa Parks

She lived over a hundred years ago, but today the old men and old women who remember her, tell of her influential life. After the Civil War, as young teen, she and her young brother, Buddy, rode their horses for a week or more to get through the woods from their home in Gilmer to Sulphur Springs. It was a difficult trip because Reconstruction Officers were monitored travelers by both horse and by train. Their mother had died just after an army comrade brought word of their father's death from pneumonia as he was on his way home from the war. An aunt, who lived in Sulphur Springs, insisted they come to live with her.

Fannie grew tall and strong, with high cheek bones, inherited, no doubt, from her father's mother who was a Cherokee Indian. She loved music, flowers, and books – all integral parts of her life.

It was her love of music that resulted in her meeting the man who would become her husband. This is how that happened. Soon after she reached Sulphur Spring, she learned that there was to be a special singing school at a local church. She immediately made plans to attend. On the very first day she met the handsome young teacher of the school, Andrew Nolen Smith. He was the eldest son of the Valentine Smith Family of the Barker Springs (Sherley) community. Andy was good-looking, light-skinned, with dark hair and a receding hair line. She thought he was handsome, but because he was some years older than she, she feared he would take no notice of her. She need not have worried, because Andy Smith was soon giving her lots of attention, and when the school was over, he came courting! Right away they found that their mutual love of all things musical would be a basis for a life together.

They were married in 1881 and lived for a time in Sulphur Springs on West Main Street. Andy worked as manager of the Pearson Music Company. Soon, however, they decided they could do better farming. So they moved to a place just across the road from his parents' home in Barker Springs. This location had the added benefit of a job for Fanny, for she was hired to be the local Postmaster.

Ten of their eleven children were born in that community, but after his parents died, they bought a farm about seven miles southwest Sulphur Springs. The deep sandy soil in that area was just right for growing all sorts of fruits and vegetables: watermelons, sweet potatoes, beans, peas, and strawberries. This produce was marketed in Sulphur Springs. Their house was a typical one of the time – a wide, deep porch all across the front with a hall running from its center to a back porch. Double doors made it possible to close off the hallway. There were three rooms on the left and two on the right. A huge magnolia tree centered the front yard with flowers growing everywhere; pot plants lined the porches and sent their flowering vines up and across the porch ceiling.

The family grew rapidly in the early years of their marriage. First there was Jenny McMaster, then Joe Valentine, followed by Alice Annie, James Hiram, Albert Nolen, Andrew, Robert Lowry, William Leroy, Mary Frances, Grace, and finally Gordon. Many women would have found the care of all those children, plus helping with the farm, to be all any one person could do. But not Fanny! She was no longer eligible to work at the post office after her first child was born, but she led a full and productive life. For example, she always made time for reading – she read while she churned, she read while she tended children and grandchildren, and she read after they had all gone to bed. She liked poetry, the classics, and the latest fiction. "Grandma always read her books twice," a grand-daughter said "first for the story, and second, for the beauty of the writing." She made each visit to her house special. "Suggy," she might say to one of the grand-daughters, "Let's make a cake for dinner." "There was," the grand-daughter continued, "always something fun to do at Grandma's; she always had time for us."

She painted, played the piano, and was a master gardener. And she was a great influence on generations of her descendants. For those who would learn, she taught them to play the piano; for those loved books, she provided a generous supply; for those who loved beauty in nature, she involved them in her gardening. And she was determined to see that those who would go, would also get a college education.

Music was always a big part of the Smith's family life. On Sundays they loaded their small pump organ into the farm wagon and went far and near to "singings." Andrew took his horn, as well, and he and Fanny were in demand at the community gatherings because they not only played music but they sang beautifully as well. (Because there was usually a baby in the family, or a baby on the way, Fanny was not always able to go with Andrew. In those cases, he went alone, for he could never resist a singing.)

Every day, throughout the year, Fanny worked some in her yard.

Grafting, rooting, potting, planting, she produced a yard full of flowers, as well as pot plants, sharing them generously with friends, family, and neighbors. She studied gardening methods and built a large, deep "flower pit" to protect her plants from the cold Texas winters.

In the spring of 1917, a dark cloud brought a cyclone (tornado) through the community, blowing away houses and barns. The Smith's saw it coming and took shelter in Grandma's "flower pit." Although the storm blew through their path, none of them was injured!

One of her granddaughters said, "Grandma was never idle. She started her day early, and soon after daylight she could be seen in the garden, working among her flowers. Later in the day, if she had company, or if she visited someone in their home, she did 'handwork' – crochet or embroidery. After all, Grandma was reared in the time of spinning wheels and home looms for making cloth. She had her own spinning wheel, cotton cards, and loom. In order to make space for this work, she had a room made at the end of the back porch called the weaving room."

One of her grand-daughters remembers helping her pick seeds out of cotton she had picked from the family farm in order to spin and then weave cloth for various family needs. She usually dyed the cloth she had spun. For example, she used the hulls from black walnuts to dye linings for her quilts.

Caring for so many children was a demanding job, and although Fanny and Andrew successfully reared nine fine young people, their lives were not without problems. Early on, when there were just two babies – Jenny, age three, and Joe, age one, - there was a life threatening accident. One cold winter day, Fanny secured baby Joe in his highchair and placed it near the fireplace in the front room. While little Jenny played nearby, Fanny went into the kitchen for something that she needed for cooking over the front room fireplace. Before she could get back into the front room she heard a terrible scream. Dashing back to the babies, she found the highchair overturned with baby Joe's head lying on red-hot coals in the edge of the fire. He survived the terrible burn, but never regained sight in his left eye.

One child, Andrew, died in infancy, and another, Albert, died at thirteen. And a few years later, the family suffered the death of their beloved Leroy. He was 29, and scheduled to leave home soon to go away to school – the first one of them to go to college – when he suddenly suffered an attack of appendicitis that was fatal.

Fanny was never too busy to help her children and grandchildren and they all loved her dearly. Through the years, they passed down many stories about her and her life. For example, her oldest son, Joe, lived on a farm across the road from her home, so she saw his children often. And, of course, she was always ready to help when one of the children was sick. There was the time when the oldest one, Ewell, had double pneumonia, and the doctor said he was not likely to survive the night. There was only one possible way to save him, the doctor said. They were to make a tent over his bed and keep it filled with steaming water for him to breathe it all through the night. Fanny was there and she said, "We can do it!" And they did; they brought in a wash tub, set it under the tent that they made over the sick-bed, and throughout the night they filled it with teakettles of hot water. Into this hot tub they put hot stones heated in the fireplace. As the night ended. The doctor said he would live.

Another time one of her daughters got a serious case of double pneumonia just as her baby was to be born. "What could they do with an infant and no mother to nurse it?" Fanny said, "I'll take it home with me and feed it until her mother can nurse her." The baby was born on a cold, icy day, but Grandma wrapped it in warm blankets and carried it to her house. Right away there was a problem finding milk that the baby's little stomach could tolerate – not cows' milk, not goats' milk, nor canned milk. But Fanny she did not give up. Finally, she tried Eagle Brand Sweetened Condensed Milk, weakening it with warm water, and it suited the baby just fine! They raised her on that until she was able to eat table foods.

As the years passed there were various illnesses and Fanny always helped when extra nursing was needed for her children or grandchildren. In the great flu epidemic of 1919, Faye almost died, and Grandma came and stayed to help with the nursing until the fever "broke" and they knew Faye would get well. Then there was Howard, who shot himself in the thumb with his air gun. Dr. Pickett came to remove the bullet and in an effort to reduce the pain, he gave Howard chloroform - too much chloroform. After the doctor left, hours passed and Howard did not wake. Edith called Grandma to ask what should be done. Grandma rushed to the house and found Howard still sleeping, so she quickly stood him on his head! When that did not help she said, "We must get Dr. Pickett quickly or this boy will die!" Fortunately the doctor was in and he rushed to the home and in the nick of time Howard was saved!

Despite various problems, the greatest tragedy of them all struck the family in 1916 - before the youngest children were grown. It happened one hot summer day. Andy had grown a large crop of watermelons that year. In fact, his farm was known for producing some of the largest melons in the county. That day, he had taken a wagon full of them to market. The huge melons sold quickly and after a few other chores, he started home. It was a busy time and he was anxious to get back to the fields to gather another load of produce for the next day's market. But alas, it was not to be. Somewhere along the way home, Andrew suffered a fatal heart attack. Nobody ever knew exactly how it happened but about one in the afternoon, Fanny heard the wagon roll up to the front porch and stop. She waited, expected

Andrew to come in the front door. After a few minutes when that didn't happened, she went outside. It was a strange and unsettling sight to see Andrew in the wagon seat, leaning backward as if he could not move. What could be wrong? She moved closer and stepping up on the wagon rail, she touched him. Then she quickly called out for help. Gordon and the others at home at the time came running and lifted him from the wagon onto a porch chair. But there was no help for him - somewhere along the way he had died. The mules, without any guidance, had pulled the wagon home! Andrew was gone quickly - at age sixty-one! - leaving a big farm, a wife and several of the children still at home! In an effort to show the respect that people had for Andy and his family, the Sulphur Springs Gazette reported that there were 38 wagons and other vehicles that followed the hearse from the home to the Sherley church and cemetery.

In 1924, when only two children were left at home, Franny rented a house in Sulphur Springs and moved there so that the children could go to a high school. When they graduated, she sold the farm and bought a boarding house in Commerce. There Grace and Gordon could go to college and their mother could support them by taking in boarders!

In 1929, Fanny was moving a piece of furniture in her hallway, when she tripped and fell, hitting her head. She never regained consciousness, dying October 8, 1929. The family buried her, beside her husband. In her obituary that was published in the Sulphur Springs Gazette, the editor noted that people in county "would remember, Mrs. A .N. Smith, for she was, for many years, the correspondent from the Liberty Community. She used the pen name, Susie Ann."

Children, Grandchildren, Great-grandchildren, even Great-Great-Great-Grandchildren speak of her with love and wonder. People who know the family say, "The Smith women get their energies from Fanny Picket, and, if they are lucky, a sprinkling of her many talents."

LONG AGO GRANDMOTHER

Before paved roads; before frozen foods; before automobiles.

Grandmother, born at the end of the Victorian Age, lived out her life in a small rural community in northeast Texas. No highways, no radios, no frozen foods, no commercial enterprise in her village except for the general store. The isolated farming community was, like many across the nation in the years of the 1920s and 30s, seriously affected by the "great depression."

Grandmother was a big woman, stern, matter-of-fact, seldom demonstrative, hard-working, but committed to her family and her local community. She helped her husband in the corn and cotton fields, and sent her four children to the local grammar school, clean and dressed in the clothing she had sewn for them. She fed them from the family's vegetable gardens and orchards with, of course, eggs and milk and butter from their own animals. Not considering herself poor in any way, she was quick to help others who were "less fortunate."

She was one of those rare people who people said could "stop blood." This made her much in demand when someone in the community had had a bad accident or had an extended nosebleed. Could she really stop an injured body from bleeding? Who's knows? however, folklore tells of people like her throughout the pioneering days of this country. When called to a victim, Grandmother took her Bible, went to the home, asked to see the victim alone. There she read a specific verse from the Bible and said a prayer. She assured the patient that the bleeding would stop, and in all the reported cases, the bleeding had stopped by the time she left the home.

She was also in demand as the local midwife. With twenty miles over dirt roads between a doctor and the community, most babies were born long before a medical man arrived. She carried some special supplies to a birthing. Among them was a sack of onions. These she set to boiling when she arrived, and by the time the baby was born, she fed the new mother a cup of onion broth to relax her and send her into a restful sleep.

She was always responsive when they was a death among the neighbors. Of course there were no restaurants or places to buy prepared foods in those rural areas, so it was essential that women of the community feed the visiting relatives of the family. Sometimes, that was for several days, especially if family members had to come a great distance for the funeral. Once in talking about those times, she said, "It was often a challenge; I remember that sometimes in the depths of the Depression, we fed them with chicken and dumplings that we made without any chicken!"

Puzzled, we asked: "How would you do that?"

"Oh, we just used lots of butter and black pepper," she replied.

During the Depression there was a stream of tramps who traveled the countryside, looking for work – and for something to eat. When one of them knocked on her back door, she always responded positively, "sit right here on the steps and I will bring you a plate." When the man finished eating the generous plate of food she gave to him, s he would say, "If you have time, you might chop a small stack of stove wood for me, then I will have food cooked for the next person who needs a meal." Almost everyone one of them stayed to produce some stove wood for her. After all, they recognized an angel when they saw one!

Chapter III

Religion in our Lives

BUILDING A CHURCH

building for eternity...

In 1898, with the turn of the century approaching, the folks in our small rural village of 300 or so, decided it was time for the community to have a real church house.

The area had been settled in the 1840s by a large extended family of Burns from Scotland. They, of course, were Scots Presbyterians. As time passed, others moved into the area giving it an ecumenical population that included not only those faithful Presbyterians, but also Methodist, Church of Christ, and Baptists. Each of those groups had worship services in the community's only public building - the school house. In fact, in 1868, when Franklin Marrs gave the land for the school house, he stipulated that it was to be used on Sundays for worship services, with the local denominational groups taking turns leading the services each Sunday.

Early in the 1870s – not long after the Civil War ended – a powerful Methodist preacher, known as EBD Johnson, moved into the community and continued his calling to organize Methodist churches. The first one was in the local community. It grew rapidly and by the 1890s the congregation led the effort to build a church – a Methodist church that would share its space with other denominations in the community. Everyone in the entire area wanted to be a part of project.

Now the largest landowners in the area were the Corbet Family and they came forward immediately with the offer of land for the church. They would give the back end of their farm – land which was across the road from the school house.

Almost immediately there were offers from every quarter. For example, every Methodist man offered to work on the actual building; every Methodist woman signed on to the crew that would paper the walls once the building was constructed. The Burns Family owned many acres of "bottom" land where the huge oak trees grew, and they gave trees for the foundation of the building – agreed not only to give the trees, but to cut them down and get them sawed into appropriate sizes for the building. A handicapped man, Mr. Walter Johnson, who was not able to climb or do carpentry work, offered to drive his farm wagon to Jefferson, Texas, to get the building materials that were not available locally. (He made this trip many times before the work was completed.)

They decided to use the New England style for the church with a capacity of seating for about 200. That design was characterized by a steep roof on a rectangular building with two front doors. This arrangement of doors made it possible for men to enter by one door and women to enter by the other one. Four windows on each side allowed for beauty of design and for plenty of light for daytime services.

They were concerned about light for the evening services. Nowhere in the community was there any form of lighting other than coal oil lamps. But, oh my, how they wished for better lighting. Finally one of the members came forward with the idea of installing a new invention called carbide lights. They were expensive, but they provided lights almost as effective as electric ones. They considered their costs, their availability and finally made the decision to invest in them. Again, Mr. Johnson took his wagon to Jefferson to buy these precious additions to the building.

Of course, it took several months to complete the building because they could work on the church only at the times when their farms did not require their attention. Everyone had a job. Some were good at carpentry, some at painting, some at roofing, but together they made a beautiful building – the pride of the community!

One day as the group was roofing the building there was a terrible accident with the potential for serious injury when Mr. Renshaw was working on the roof. For some reason even he could not explain, he turned his foot and went tumbling off that tall building landing on a pile of lumber in the church yard. Oh, but it was frightening – other workers stood as if paralyzed to see such a thing happen. Surely he would be dead by the time they turned him over. They raced toward him, only to see the young Mr. Renshaw stand, stretch himself, and climb back upon the roof. The shingling continued. On-lookers breathed again and they all lived to tell this remarkable tale. This incident assured the people that the Lord was with them!

Inside, the walls of the building were papered with cream colored paper and the ceiling was painted with a complementary color. Furnishings include a pulpit, a table for the altar and two chairs. An attractive railing surrounded the altar area. Pews fit into three linear sections. But the most valued of all the furnishings was a fine new organ!

A great, tall steeple was the building's crowning glory.

The church was completed in 1899, but they waited until the turn of the century for the dedication ceremony. Folks said more than a thousand people came for the services. They packed into the pews and stood around the walls. When there was no more standing room, they stood outside at the open windows. After the service, there was dinner on the ground followed by afternoon of singing. It was a great celebration!

An update: In 2000, the community celebrated the 100th anniversary of the building. Sometime just before that event, they had hired a professional in church restoration to strengthen the foundation and the entire structure. In the 1950s they had reworked the front of the church, adding an entrance that accommodates a set of double doors rather than the two single ones. Earlier, too, they had added an extension to hold a kitchen, dining room, bathrooms, and children's Sunday School rooms. For the 100th anniversary, brass lighting fixtures and stained glass windows were added in honor of deceased members.

The building, now, as then, is the pride of the community!

A GIFT FROM THE HEART

...and a poor widow came and put in two coins...

Mark 12: 22

Down on the farm, in the days of Early America, animals were critical to a family's livelihood. The horses for riding and pulling farm machinery; cows for milk, cream and butter; and pigs for pork to eat throughout the cold winter months. Likewise, the lowly chicken was important not only to provide Sunday dinners, but because the mature ones laid eggs for the family's daily meals. Without them there was no cornbread, no cake, no potato salad, and even worse, no fried eggs for the essential "farmer's breakfast!"

The farm wife had another reason for giving special attention to her flock, for they, along with cream from the cows, provided the only cash money that was hers alone. You see, in pioneering times, it was a time-honored custom that monies from the sale of extra chickens, eggs, butter and cream belonged to the wife!

Therefore, the prudent wife gave daily attention to her flock of chickens, being careful to put aside one or two eggs each day so that when nature caused a hen to take to her nest, there would be 21 eggs to put under her for hatching into more baby chicks in just a few weeks. Woe to the wife who did not have eggs to place under a hen when the creature decided to go into the "setting" mode. Often farm women shared with others when there was a need for a "setting" (21) of eggs.

My grandmother told a story about a setting of eggs. The story came about in their rural and remote village when a visiting preacher announced that on the following Sunday he would return and bring the equipment needed for celebrating the sacrament of communion. That was a rare service which was highly valued and which was seldom offered in their remote village.

The appointed Sunday came and the church was packed. The minister preached a stirring sermon about the gift of the Christ Child and his gift of love and forgiveness. Then the people were invited to knee at the altar for communion. The front of the church could barely hold them as they all knelt in this sacred moment.

My grandmother said, "You will not believe what happened at that service. I was never so embarrassed. Old Lady Pickens, who lives way off down there in the bottom and never has an extra penny to her name, knelt next to me. As we rose to return to our seats she said in a loud whisper – could be heard all around, "Aunt Lola, I have a setting of Dominaker hen eggs for you if you can use 'em!"

My grandmother said she was horrified. "Imagine - just imagine" she would say – "that a person would say something like that at the end of such a high spiritual moment." As we were growing up she told this story often to impress on us the importance of taking communion as a holy practice.

But, in retrospect, I think my grandmother may have had it wrong. Maybe Old Mrs. Pickins was so moved by the service, that she wanted to give to her friend the only thing she had to give – a setting of hen eggs!

HISTORY OF A METHODIST CHURCH

...on this rock I will build my church.

Methodists love to talk of their history! In fact, they say their movement began with Jesus Christ, but of course a lot of significant events occurred between his time and ours!

They begin by explaining how in early Texas – when it was first owned by Spain and later by Mexico – only the Catholic religion was allowed. The Spanish presence was brought here first by the priests who were sent to build Mission Guadalupe (1716). They said their purpose was to make Christians of the local Indians but they were also very hopeful that these East Texas missions would keep the French from taking over this property - then claimed by Spain!. Although the attempts by the Catholic missionaries continued for some time, eventually they were judged to be less than successful because even though the Indians would come into the missions for a while, they would eventually return to their own East Texas homes. Some years after the missions were closed; there came enough Spanish settlers to the area for the Catholic Church to establish a diocese. Their first church was just one block from downtown. Decades later they built further out, and today they have an enormous plant near the edge of town.

Protestants have a different story. In the first years of East Texas settlements, the only Protestant worship services were in secret. As a result there are records of only one or two such services. Certainly the Protestants had no buildings until after Texas gained independence from Mexico in 1936. But immediately after independence was secured, protestant missionaries came from the States. In Nacogdoches there were first the Baptists who established the country church north of town called "Old North Church," but soon there with others – especially Methodists and Presbyterians.

Local long-time Methodists speak of their history with pride of place and with interesting stories collected from their 178 years. Ask one of them and they will say, "Well of course, our beginnings were with Jesus

Christ, from whom all Christian Churches originated." Sunday school teachers explain about the great persecution of early Christians; about the gradual acceptance of Christianity after the conversion of the government leader. They speak of the development of the Roman Church - then the break-away of a group we know as Eastern Orthodox. They explain how hundreds of years of change occurred with the leadership of such men as Saint Peter of Ireland, St. Frances of Assisi, Martin Luther of Germany and others. The thinking and leadership of these devote Christians resulted in the Reformation and in the division of the Christian Church in the western world into Catholics and Protestants and the further establishment of the Church of England.

Methodists were not planned as a denomination; rather members began as a group within The Church of England. The movement began with a young seminary student named John Wesley, son of a Church of England minister and his wife Suzanna, who herself was a great Christian leader and teacher. Wesley was motivated by the plight of the great hordes of poor people in England – by their terrible working conditions and by the generations of children who worked in factories and mines without benefit of education. As a young university student Wesley recruited others to study the problems of the poor and to find ways to address them. They began by going to the mine sites and preaching to the men and boys as they came up from the depths of those mines. They also looked for other places to preach to the people wherever they were – usually out of doors – and a new concept was born - OUTDOOR PREACHING!

Eventually the group initiated another new concept: ORGANIZING LAYMEN TO DO SOME OF THE PREACHING – men who did not have the education for a full-time minister but who could share the gospel and work with the people under the direction of an experienced minister. (Baptists, too, used this concept as they organized churches in America.)

Wesley then conceived the idea of teaching the people on Sundays in a school that focused on reading and writing. Those who had never learned to read could come on Sundays and learn to read - AND SO BEGAN SUNDAY SCHOOLS!

The Wesleyan Movement grew and eventually the groups were called "Methodists" because of their careful organization and their methodical work habits.

When Oglethorpe brought men from the crowded prisons in England to settle in Georgia, he asked John Wesley to come to establish churches within the new state. He did come and although he was less than successful in the new world he did establish a system of Circuit Riders that resulted in Methodist churches all over the new world. Folklores says that right behind every wagon train in Early America was a Methodist Circuit Rider.

Of course the Methodist Circuit Riders were not welcome – not legal!– until Texas gained independence from Mexico. However, Methodist missionaries from the states were poised to come to Texas just as soon as independence was won. That happened in 1836, and the call went out for missionaries who would like to be assigned to this new country called Texas. Littleton Fowler was a young minister in Tennessee when he heard the call, and he immediately volunteered to come. The bishop sent him directions for coming from his parish in Tennessee to Texas: *First, buy a horse! Then start from Memphis by steamboat to Natchez. Travel by land from Natches to Natchitoches – thence to San Augustine and then to Nacogdoches.*

The directions were all right, but young Mr. Fowler knew a more direct route – through the Oklahoma Territory to Clarksville; thence to Nacogdoches, and later, on to San Augustine. He preached first in Clarksville, but he was soon in Nacogdoches. Here he held a revival and 18 people came forward to begin a "Methodist Society." The 18 began immediately to raise funds for a church house, but alas, what they raised was insufficient for a building, so they did, as others were to do – held their services every Sunday in homes or public buildings such as the court house.

In due time, young Mr. Fowler met and married a widow here in Nacogdoches. (She was widowed when her husband was killed by a bear.) This marriage got Littleton in a bit of trouble with his bishop because, as news is wanted to do, some of his activities were distorted by the time they were reported to the bishop. It seems that when Littleton married Ms. Porter she owned more than 4000 acres of Texas land - this from her deceased husband who had been a land speculator. When the story got to the bishop it sounded as if Littleton might have been doing some land dealing. As a result, the bishop sent a hot letter to all three Texas missionaries saying: "the only reason for missionaries to be in Texas is to save souls and establish churches. I want to hear no more about land speculation!"

In 1860, the Methodists were able to use a small building which sat at the corner of North Pecan and Hospital Streets for their services. The little building was only 24' by 36' feet and in just a few years, the society outgrow it. Members decided it was time to build a real church building.

They bought the lot across the street (where the present sanctuary is located) and build in The New England style – much like the of Old North Church. They were able to sell the small building to a man who moved it to the lot that he owned just west of the present sanctuary. There he set it up for his residence. One winter evening as he cooked his supper, he accidently started a grease fire in his kitchen and not only did his home (the little old church building) burn to the ground, but so did the new church!

Of course they rebuild, and this time they were able to have a design created by the now-famous local architect, Diedrich Rulfs. Historians call it the 1910 church and it was much loved. Its design was popular at the time – a semi circularly sanctuary that allowed congregants to see more of the people in the pews. It gave them all a sense of closeness to the altar. However some years after WWII (1969) that church was razed and the present one was built on its site. According to their long-range plan, the sanctuary wing was attached to the education wing which had been built in 1952. In 1987 and in 2015 there were additions of a family life center, more education space, and (later) an enlarged youth center and children's area.

Much earlier, in 1902, the women of the church had raised funds to build and furnish a parsonage which they located on the site of the present chapel. A few years later they had the use of a larger house on Mound Street until they built a new parsonage on at the end of Raguet Street. Members of Methodist Women raised funds to furnish it, too. It continues to be the resident parsonage.

The congregation that began with 18 people now has 1200 or so members and constituents. With active programs of worship, study, and service, local folks say the church has excellent leadership from Senior Pastor, Dr. Jeff McDonald. Programs for seniors, youth, adults and children thrive as they carry the church into the community of Nacogdoches.

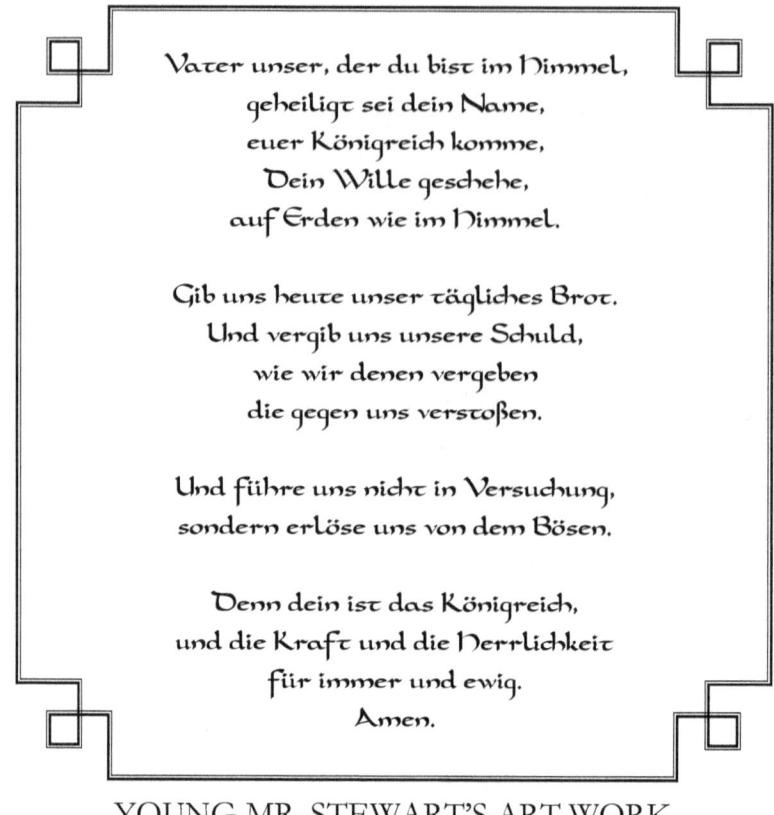

YOUNG MR. STEWART'S ART WORK

...it is something to be able to paint a picture...
Henry David Thoreau

In the bell tower of the First United Methodist Church, Nacogdoches, there hangs a piece of art work that few can explain. Some years ago it was found, setting on the floor, in the corner of one of the church's store rooms. "What is this?" asked the volunteers who were cleaning the room.

No one knew. "Well, it's right pretty," said one of them, "why don't we use it in the cluster of wall hangings we are arranging in the bell tower. It is," she continued, "large enough to center the grouping."

As they completed the rather attractive wall of pictures, one said, "Someone should find out what this artwork is." Another said, "Well, the lettering on it is obviously foreign and I believe it is German."

"You are right," said another, "and the pastor speaks German, let's ask him to look at it." Together they determined that the piece is indeed the Lord's Prayer written in German and embellished by an artist with color and shapes. But how did it come to be in the church?

Finally an older woman among them said that a former member of the church, Mrs. Mary Duncan, who died a few years ago, had German relatives still living Nacogdoches (the lady's name was Anna Katherine Holbrook.) Perhaps, they could solve the mystery. She volunteered to visit Mrs. Holbrook and learn more. Here is the story of the artwork.

In 1856, there was a young college student in Germany named Wilhelm Henrick Boeschen. He was an art major and the wall hanging in question was the result of a requirement in his freshman painting class. Now, at the time, most young German men were being conscripted for military service, and to keep their son from being drafted, the Boeschens sent Wilhelm to England. There he lived with a family who was especially kind to him, and as a result he anglicized his own name using their surname. He became William Steward.

In those years, the Civil War was raging in the United States and William decided to join that effort. For some time he served in the U.S. navy, eventually becoming a captain. At one time his ship sailed into the Galveston harbor and he became so favorably impressed with Texas that when the war ended he returned to live here, entering the state via San Augustine. There he met and married Miss Nellis Miller. The couple soon moved to Nacogdoches to establish their home. Their first baby was a girl whom they named Mary.

In Naocgdoches the young couple became acquainted with another family from Germany, the Schmidts, who were well established in East Texas. As the friendship progressed Mr. Schmidt asked William if he would like them to help him get his widowed mother to Texas. Of course he agreed and in due time the mother arrived, bringing with her William's sister and his sister's husband, Diedrich Rulfs (who became the celebrated Nacogdoches architect)!

Mary Steward grew up and married a Naogdoches man named Duncan. She worked for many years as a buyer for Schmidths and was a very active member of First United Methodist Church. After her death (at age 103) relates learned that she had kept her father's artwork all these years and had willed it to the church. At that time – some 40 years ago – her father's art was delivered to the church, but in the various processes of renovating and redecorating the building the artwork had been put away and forgotten until the ladies, working together sometime in the 1980s, rediscovered it.

Today the Boseschen artwork hangs proudly in the church's historic bell tower!

CIRCUIT RIDER

...Go and make disciples...
Matthew 28:20

Historians say that behind every wagon train that crossed America in the pioneer days there was a Methodist Circuit Rider. These men were preachers sent to organize churches in pioneer towns. In Texas, the circuit riders made their first appearance after the people gained independence from Mexico, because, of course, only the Catholic Church was allowed when the territory belonged to Spain and later to Mexico. The presence of the Circuit Riders was especially strong following the Civil War when many families from the Deep South who suffered from destruction of their farms and plantations moved west to "start over" in Texas. One of the many circuit riders of that era was Erasmus Berestifer Dow Johnson. This is a portion of his story.

Known in his adult life as "EBD," he was born in 1821, in Wilkes County North Carolina to Henry and Sally Green Johnson. EBD lived in the time of Abraham Lincoln and Andrew Johnson, both U.S. Presidents during the Civil War. His family moved from North Carolina to Tennessee, and then to Arkansas - always looking for more and better land. Soon after they settled in Arkansas, EBD's father died of pneumonia, leaving the young sons to work the farm. One day while EBD was chopping wood, the ax slipped, cutting a deep gash in his leg. As often happened, gangrene set in and the leg had to be amputated just below the knee. His mother bought a peg leg for him, but in time, he designed and carved a better one for himself. It had a "rocker" rather than a peg, making it possible for him to walk at a faster pace.

As a teen he went to a camp meeting and there he felt the call to spread the gospel throughout the frontier. With the guidance of an experienced Methodist minister, he began preaching right away, serving first in northern Louisiana, then in southern Arkansas and finally in northeast Texas.

In Louisiana he met and married the pretty little black-haired French girl, Martha Jane DeMoss. They settled on a farm in Arkansas where he continued working with communities to establish Methodist churches. As he traveled, if he came to a community that had no school, he would organize one and teach a 3-month term. He stayed nights with families in the communities, spending evenings tutoring the children. Oddly enough, he carried a couple of "shoe lasts" in his saddlebags and if children in the family needed shoes, he made them during those long winter evenings.

Near the end of the war, soldiers swept through Arkansas demolishing everything in their path, including the Johnson farm. When the burning and destruction were over, the only things the family had left were the things they had hidden in the woods. Like many, they decided to relocate in Texas. They packed all their belongings in one covered wagon. Then, tying their cow to the back of the wagon, they set off.

Weeks passed and one day their baby was so sick they decided to make camp early. The mother no longer produced baby's milk, and the cow had died, so they had nothing to satisfy the hungry baby. As soon as they stopped for the night EBD gave the two oldest boys coins and asked them to go along the road until they found a house and buy milk for the baby. Leaving the mother to start a fire for the evening, he went with his gun into the woods to seek a squirrel or perhaps a rabbit to cook for their evening meal. Way after dark, the boys returned, empty-handed. In that troubled time after the war, people were simply too afraid of strangers to let them near.

That night their baby died.

The next morning they buried her and then they packed up to move on. "We will not stay in a community," EBD said, "that has no welcome for strangers or no milk for babies."

In another community not far away they found a suitable farm for sale and established a home that would be the seat of their family for generations to come. Neighbors helped build a log cabin and EBD began his rounds. That first year in Texas he traveled 1700 miles, receiving a salary from the Methodist organization of $85.00. He preached the Wesley themes of practical Christianity:

DO NO HARM
DO ALL THE GOOD YOU CAN
STAY CLOSE TO GOD.

Of course, he preached against the deadly sins of owning slaves, liquor, dancing, and gambling.

Tales of his ministry are endless – inspiring, interesting, sad - even funny. His family of ten children provided challenges along with the challenges of keeping all those churches active. For example, the oldest daughter eloped with a man of questionable standards and she was not in touch with the family for two or three years, knowing that her father would not allow a man like her husband into the family. Finally, one day they received a post card from her. It said:

Dear Pa and Ma. My husband died several weeks ago and I am cooking the last beans today. I am near Fort Worth at.......

Love,
Jane

"Boys," said EBD to his two teenage sons, "Boys, we must get her home! Soon they hitched horses to the wagon and the two teen sons left for Fort Worth loaded with food for the horses and for themselves, along with funds to buy essentials for Jane and her babies. During the three weeks it required to get there and back, EBD and his church members raised a log cabin for Jane and her children on the grounds of the family home. It was a great day when the boys returned with her to the care of the family.

Less poignant, but another well-remember story happened one night after the family was in bed. Martha and EBD were sleeping in a bed beside a shuttered window – EBD of course sleeping in long johns with his peg leg on the floor beside the bed. As they slept, there came a frantic knocking at the window. EBD rose on his knees, and opening the shutters, he found a couple on horseback. "Marry us as quick as you can preacher," said the young man. "Do you have a license?" EBD asked. The girl handed him a paper and pencil. He signed it; handed it back; and said, "Join hands. I pronounce you man and wife."

With a strike to the horse's hips, the couple raced away. EBD closed the shutter and lay back in bed, but before they were asleep there was a great sound of galloping horses rushing past the house.

"Martha," said EBD, as they sank into sleep, "I guess we have just married another run-away couple."

EBD Johnson preached for fifty years and, with his wife, raised eight of those ten children, was a faithful husband, and a strong force in the establishment of the faith community. When he died in 1889, his biographer reported that he had established forty-four Methodist churches.

REMEMBERING BISHOP HOUSTON

...It is wonderful how much can be done if we are always doing.
                                                      Thomas Jefferson

The family's research has led his children to believe that their father, Bishop Walter B. Houston was the oldest minister in Texas who was still pastoring a church when he died a few years ago at age 97. Although his pastorate was in Tyler, Texas, Nacogdoches people know him because his wife of 29 years was Ms. Maudie May Davis Houston, a local lady. Bishop Houston's work and accomplishments were prenominal – worth hearing his story!

He was born to a working family of African Americans in Tyler, Texas. The young family had a good start with the father working for the railroads and the mother caring for their three little boys. Nevertheless, troubles came. First, one of the boys was killed in an accident when their buggy overturned as the family traveled to their relatives home outside of Tyler. Then, with cutbacks at the railroad, the father lost his job. Next, beyond all belief, the father disappeared while he was looking for work in Dallas. When days and weeks without word from him passed the mother set about finding ways to support herself and the two boys. She returned to Tyler where she supported herself and the boys by taking in laundry. Day after day, people brought their laundry to her, and day by day she spent her hours washing dirty clothes. When they were dried and ironed the two boys delivered them to the customer.

The boys were always helpful to their mother and they did well in school. Early on, young Walter B. decided he wanted to be a minister, and with the help of a local preacher-mentor, he began studies toward that goal. He excelled in his work and quickly became a preacher in demand. Other the years he became known as "Bishop Houston," an important designation in his denomination. He was energetic and resourceful: preaching, working part-time, and caring for his own family that, over time, included ten children. His main pastorate was in Tyler, but he served as an evangelist to congregations throughout East Texas .

In the early days, he often preached out of doors on vacant lots. The people who came to hear him sat on upended wooden boxes obtained from the "discard" pile at the railroad where many of the men worked. A platform and lectern were built from similar materials. Services were often at night with bottle lights – dangerous, perhaps, but making the late services possible. People came; they liked the preaching; and they felt the Holy Spirit. The gentle East Texas breezes provided the only air conditioning they needed, and the chirping of the birds contributed to their singing. That first outdoor church created a feeling of closeness to the Lord himself. One member said, "Looking up to the blue sky above us made me feel we were at the very gates of heaven."

So many people joined the congregation that a real building was needed. With the depression in full swing, there was little hope of buying building materials, but Bishop Houston was firm in his belief that "the Lord makes a way." He prayed often and fervently, and he used his creative mind to help the Lord "provide." This is a story about how he, and the Lord, grew their first little church building. Again, the Boxcar Shop discards became the source of lumber for the building. Among the discarded items from the refurbishment of boxcars were wooden boxcar doors - each one 6 feet by 8 feet . Those big strong doors became the church walls. After setting up a frame for the building, they were attached to all sides, thus making an enclosure. Their dimensions dictated the size of the building: 24' x 36'. But what could they do for a roof? They considered many materials – all too costly. Then they remembered the heavy thick fabrics used to make sacks for cotton pickers – 'duckin' it was called. With that ingenious idea, Walter figured how much fabric would be needed to cover the entire building; then he approached a local dry goods store that agreed to sell whole bolts of the fabric to the congregation at a greatly reduced cost. Back home with the heavy material, Walter, and his brother Alex, moved their mother's sewing machine into the backyard and the three cut and sewed until they had materials to fit over the top frame of the entire building.

Of course they needed lights if they were to have the evening services that were so important to a congregation of working people. Sadly, they discovered that there was absolutely no money for bringing electricity to the building. Finally, Bishop Houston said, "We will just have to turn this problem over to the Lord." And with that they began services – all in the day time.

The first service was held on a fine summer Sunday. The singing and preaching lasted well into the afternoon. People felt the Lord was with them; in fact they felt the Holy Spirit literally filled the place. Someone else felt the Lord was there too, for on Monday, as Walter B. moved about the empty building picking up trash and cleaning the place, a little old lady came quietly into the building. She timidly approached Walter and said "Brother Houston, I'm Mrs. Mayfield. I live next door and yesterday I watched your service all day from my front porch. I listened to the singing and preaching, and the Lord has put into my heart a feeling that you need something I have. Its electricity. I want to lend you some of my electric power so that you can have night services. She continued, "I have a long extension cord and we will just plug it into my front room outlet. Then, with an 100 watt bulb, you will have enough light to have services after dark."

"Hallelujah!" shouted Walter, as he reached to hug the old lady. "The Lord does make a way!"

Bishop Houston told that story over and over in the years to come as he spoke of the presence of God in the work of his people. And the church went on – and on! In fact it is there today – it stands proudly in a fine brick structure, with a real roof, and plenty of electricity!

I first met the Houston's when family members came to talk with me about writing the bishop's biography. They arrived in a big, fine, black Cadillac with a driver and Bishop Houston in the front seat and Mrs. Houston and one of the eldest daughters in the back seat. They came for a lengthy interview and with a stack of notes, papers, and other sources of information about their lives. I agreed to do the work and immediately began a year of interviews, research, and visits to his churches. During all that time I wondered how the fine big car fit into their lifestyle. Finally I asked, and this is the story I learned.

The Houston's had a strong belief that success is built on faith, family, education, and hard work. Toward that end, each of the ten children was sent to Texas College, and each received degrees – some later obtained advanced degrees. Of course tuition for that many children was often difficult to come by. When a semester began and there was not enough money for tuition, Bishop Houston would visit the college president to see what might be done to keep the young people in college. The president, Professor Glass, made a standing agreement with the bishop. The students could attend classes "on credit" but the loans must be paid before they could "walk across the stage" (i.e. graduate). One year there were three Houston children ready to graduate, and the bill for their tuition was considerable. Again the bishop visited the president but there was no change in the agreement.

"I just cannot, in all honesty, allow students to graduate who have not paid the tuition that is absolutely required for college students, Bro. Houston," said Professor Glass. "I think you can understand that the college won't last long if we don't collect tuition."

"Of course, I understand," replied Bishop Houston, "I just don't know what I am going to do to get this much money." And he went away with a heavy heart and big problem to solve. Though the night he prayed and anguished over the problem. Finally he slept, trusting in the Lord to "make a way."

As the morning light began to filter through the windows he waked, knowing what he must do. Now the bishop always worked a big garden on the large plot behind their house and there he also keeps chickens, hogs, and a team of mules. These produced eggs, milk, butter, and cream for the family and for sale to help support the growing family. It was these resources that he considered when he was deciding how to pay the big college bill and thus make graduation possible for his eldest children.

Many years later, the oldest daughter came home from her prestigious job in California to visit her father in Tyler. One afternoon she and a sister said they were going downtown to do a bit of shopping. They had not been gone long when there was a call to Bishop Houston from a local car dealer. "Bishop," the salesman said, "I wonder if you would like to come down and look at our new cars."

"Oh no," responded Bishop Houston," I am not in the market for a new car. My Buick is only ten years old and is still running fine." The caller persisted and was only able to get the bishop's agreement to come when he mentioned that he also wanted to talk with him about a church matter.

Now when Bishop Houston arrived at the car dealers, the salesman said, "Bishop, what do you think of this fine Cadillac that we are displaying this week?"

"It's very nice," said the bishop, "but as I said, I have no interest in a new car. Let's talk about the church."

At that point, there stepped from a hiding place in the showroom his two daughters. "Daddy," they asked, 'we want to know if this car could equal one farm wagon, a pair of mules, a dozen laying hens, and three hogs ready to be butchered?"

With tears in the eyes of all present, the Bishop drove home in the new Cadillac, a gift from his children – all ten college graduates!

THE REV. LITTLETON FOWLER

"Go into all the world..."
Mat. 16-15

In the early 1800s, leaders in the well-established protestant churches in the United States watched with interest as their neighbors to the southwest grappled with Mexico for control of the land called Texas. It had long offended them that only the Catholic Church was allowed to hold worship services in these lands. Occasionally a brave preacher who was not a Catholic dared to come into Texas and hold a service, but he was quickly rushed away before authorities could apprehend him.

As the Texas-Mexico conflict escalated, church leaders prepared to send missionaries to Texas just as soon as the state gained its independence from Mexico. So it is no surprise to read about a man named Littleton Fowler, who was one of three missionaries sent to Texas. A single young man, he was fully ordained to preach in the Methodist Church. Historians Carolyn Ericson and Nola Boles wrote of his work in Texas. They spoke of his physique, a tall man with the appearance of great strength. He and another man, John Denton, an associate, preached first in Clarksville, then made haste to the larger town of Nacogdoches. The trip required four days – by horseback, of course. They had all their belongings on a pack horse and at night they slept in the woods. Their first sermon in Nacogdoches was preached in 1938, in The Old Stone Fort (Fowler spoke of this as the "court house.") The service included spirited singing led by the Hon. Adolphus Sterne.

In Nacogdoches Littleton Fowler met a young widow, Missouri Lockwood Porter. Her husband had been killed by a bear in downtown Nacogdoches. Folks say the creature had been captured by a local man who brought him into town to show to people and (while no one was watching him) the bear broke his bindings and in an attempt to escape, he killed Mr. Porter.

Now the Porters had been in Nacogdoches for over ten years, engaged in successful land business. She had been an active helper to her husband,

and after his death she continued to manage the business for her young son, Symmes. Unfortunately, this story about "land speculation" became distorted as it traveled by first one person, then another, to the bishop.

Of course, the bishop was greatly disturbed to think one of his missionaries was in the land business. He wrote a scathing letter to Littleton that included these words:

"The only reason you are in Texas is to save souls and create Methodist societies. I don't want to hear another word about 'land speculation!'" Poor Littleton! However, he was soon able to clarify the situation by explaining his wife's ownership of the land. He explained to the bishop that she owned the land before their marriage and that she continued to manage it for her son.

He noted, too, in his letter to the bishop, that his wife supported him in every possible way – often traveling with him to the various communities where he preached. Thereafter he continued his work with the support of the bishop and other colleagues.

Despite his appearance of strength and good health, Littleton was often ill, and after an extended illness, he died at his home in Sabine County. He was only 42 years old. He is buried in the McMann's Chapel which was near his and Missouri's home. He left his stepson, Littleton Morris, and his and Missouri's two children, Mary and Littleton Fowler.

Folk tales abound about this good man and his contributions to the establishment and support of the Methodist Church in Texas, esp. in Nacogdoches and other East Texas communities.

Chapter IV
Early Schools

EARLY SCHOOLS IN EAST TEXAS

We have come so far from where we started...
but we are on the road to becoming better.
                                        Maya Angelou

Education came to Nacogdoches with the Friars who came in 1716 to operate the first mission – Mission Guadalupe de los Nacogdoches. Father Antonio Margil de Jesus was in charge of the educational program. Of course he, and others with him, taught in Spanish with a curriculum designed to convert the local Indians to Christianity. Today we know that they did not reach their lofty goals, but with their efforts came our first local "school."

Later, throughout the 19th century, there were individuals who established private schools in Texas towns. For example, early in our local history, citizens built a small school building on the site one block from the present downtown area. It was made of logs and about all we know about education there is that in 1825, a local man named Thomas

Jefferson Garner taught the first English-speaking classes in that building. Afterwards, Miss Elizabeth Holloway also taught there. Others, too, opened private schools as time went by. These were popular institutions because even after the establishment of public schools, early community school terms were for just a few months, so families, who could afford to do so, sent their children to private schools during the summer. These private schools were sometimes called "pay schools."

In 1821, Texas came under the authority of the Mexican Government and from that time until 1836, when Texas gained independence from Mexico, there was considerable dissatisfaction over Mexico's lack of attention to educational systems. However, the government did award four leagues of land to each of the new town schools. The five schools established in Texas were at San Antonio, Goliad, Gonzales, Austin, and Nacogdoches. The Nacogdoches one was in existence from 1826 to 1834. In 1845 when the Nacogdoches University was chartered, the four leagues of land were transferred from the town of Nacogdoches to the new Nacogdoches University.

In 1854, Texas passed laws for free public schools, but few were opened until after the Civil War. By the late 1850s the state had set up county school boards with elected superintendents to lead educational opportunities across the county. Rural schools were situated with the intent that no child would have to walk more than 2 miles to school. In 1857, there were 62 students in Nacogdoches County schools.

In those early years, there were only grammar schools in Texas communities – it would be the 1890s before the high school movement came to Texas and to our town. In the meantime, the Nacogdoches University was chartered. It provided "higher education" to older students – ones who had completed community grammar schools and whose parents could afford the cost of a private school.

The university was closed during the Civil War years and its building was used for a Confederate Hospital. After the war, and after the use of the university building by Reconstruction Officers, the school in the building was operated by the Masons (a boys-only school), then by the Catholic Church, and, still later, by Keachi College.

In the late 1890s, trustees resumed control of education in the University building and there they established a school for young children in the lower level of the building and a high school in the upper level of the building. These schools were for white students in Nacogdoches. A school for African American students was located at the east end of Bois

d. Arc Street - established as a result of federal law that towns must have a school for African Americans by 1870. At the time, a public school year was for four months.

Mr. G. I. Watkins became the first school superintendent in the Nacogdoches district. The first students to graduate from Nacogdoches high school received their high school education in the upper level of the Nacogdoches University building. At the turn of the century there were 575 pupils enrolled in local schools: 332 white students and 243 black students.

In 1903, Nacogdoches schools were incorporated and thus the establishment of The Nacogdoches Independent School District. In 2004, the new superintendent, R. F. Davis, led a drive for a bond election. It passed, and as a result, a building for the High School was constructed on Washington Square – close enough to the University building for use of both buildings. Funds from the bond election also provided for two other buildings – an elementary school on Irion Hill for white students and a school for African American students on Shawnee Street.

With the new High School in place, the old University Building became "Central Elementary." Some years later the elementary school was moved elsewhere and the university building was used for chemistry labs, agriculture labs and for storage. Finally, with considerable deterioration, it was set for demolition! Many in the town were horrified at the thought of losing this fine old building, so they began work to save it. Eventually it became a property of the school district with members of a federation of women's clubs serving as trustees. City leaders, public school leaders, and the women in the federation determined that the building would be renovated and used (at the lower level) for community gatherings and (at the upper level) for a museum dedicated to 19th century education and 19th century community.

The 20th century moved education in Nacogdoches forward at a fast pace – more new buildings, vocational education added to the curriculum, football, approval for a teachers college on North Street, free textbooks (1918), integration, and a "Demonstration School" at the new college. Nacogdoches even profited by the depression, for in the 1930s, the WPA built a new high school for the town. Today, it is known as the "White Building on Mound Street" where TJR Elementary is located.

Today (300 years after those first friars came to begin an education program for Indian children), Nacogdoches folks proudly support one high school (4A), two middle schools, six elementary schools, and an alternative school. Several private and church schools, as well as a large Head Start program, a fine City Library, and an active Boys and Girls Club after-school program, extend educational opportunities throughout the community.

Stephen F. Austin State University is a shining star in the community, with 80 majors, over 120 areas of study, five colleges and approximately 1200 students. Degrees are available at bachelors, masters, and doctoral levels.

NACOGDOCHES UNIVERSITY AND ITS BUILDING

Education is the guardian genius of democracy.
Maribeau B. Lamar

Some said it was only a pipe dream – it could never be done. "Not even a railroad here yet; how could the town get a charter from the new Republic for a university?" Critics asked! But they did; town leaders applied and with the help of locals at the new capitol in Austin, Nacogdoches University was founded with a charter granted by the Republic of Texas in 1845. The non-sectarian institution offered "higher education" for those who wished for more education than local communities provided. At the time, there were no high schools in Texas.

Classes were originally taught in various downtown buildings; however in 1859, the University moved into its own, new two-story building. Its modified Greek Revival architecture resembled the buildings of the University of Virginia. The building was situated on 21 acres of land designated as Washington Square. This location was originally the site of a Caddo Indian Village. A four-league land grant from the Republic, along with private subscriptions by community people including cash, land, lumber, pork and labor, financed the building. J. H. Cato was the architect for the building which was constructed for a cost of approximately $10,500.

When the building opened for classes in the fall of 1859, 41 male and 41 females were enrolled. They were taught in separate classes in the two large downstairs rooms. The upper level was used as an auditorium. The two small rooms downstairs were for small classes such as music, while the two small rooms upstairs were used for the president's office and for his living quarters.

As the Civil War began in 1861, universities across the South were closed, and soon the one local building was closed as well and converted to a hospital for Confederate soldiers. After the war the building housed the Resconstruction force. When the building gave up the last of its northern soldiers who had formed the Reconstruction Force in Nacogdoches, the

University reopened. Again, the critics said there would not be leaders for such an institution after the devastation of the war – "Who could repair the building and who would teach? And would the scholars come?" They asked. "Too much to hope for!" Some said.

But they did come, and for a decade its education programs were operated by various entities, first by the Catholic Church; next, by the Masons; and later by Keachie College (from Louisiana). Then in 1890 the University's trustees regained control of the program with classes for all ages. Soon the program that had once been a university, melted into a high school program.

In 1904, Nacogdoches formed a school district and held a successful bond election that enabled them to erect a high school building. It was situated just a few steps from the porch of the university building. When the building was completed, the Nacogdoches University trustees deeded the university property on Washington Square to the new local school district. From that year forward until sometime after the end of World War II in 1945, NISD used the building for various classes or (in later years) for storage. Old timers discussed the building's use when they were students – some mentioned its being their chemistry lab; others remembered it as their band hall. The agriculture students said they used it for a simplified poultry lab.

However, by 1954, the building had fallen into disrepair and the district no longer needed it. They asked the city to take it for a museum. The city, in turn, asked the women's organizations in town to form a federation for the purpose of restoring and using the building as a historical site. In 1954, members of the newly formed Nacogdoches Federation of Women's Clubs were officially made the trustees of the building. In 1960, with wide community support, the federation restored the building, leaving it on its original site with its original room configuration. It is still maintained by this group of volunteers and is used as a community gathering place as well as a museum. The museum, located on the second floor of the building, displays artifacts with three themes:

1. 19th Century Education
2. A Confederate Hospital
3. 19th Century Community Events held in the building.

Today the Old University Building is recognized as a local, state, and national treasure. It is widely used for community activities and is toured annually by hundreds of Texas history students, tourists, and local visitors. It stands as a monument to the value Nacogdoches people place on education. Its docents and caregivers say they are keeping faith with the wishes of their mothers and grandmothers!

SAM HOUSTON SPEAKS!

...Education is the guardian genius of democracy.........
M.Lamar

All Texas folklorists are steeped in Sam Houston tales. For example, people in Nacogdoches enjoy telling how, during the time when the area was a part of Mexico, Sam Houston converted to the Catholic religion in order to become a citizen and thus be eligible to buy land in Texas. He was baptized into that faith in the Sterne-Hoya House here in Nacogdoches. That house still stands on its original site just south of Main Street on Lanana Street. It is open daily, except Sundays, for visitors. When you visit, you will be standing in the very parlour where the baptism took place.

We also like to tell tales of Sam Houston's courtship of our own Anna Raguet. It was a well-known courtship here in town – what we don't know is why it ended short of marriage. We do know that they had to wait for his divorce which came in 1838. Later, when his Indian wife died, he was legally cleared to court Anna. Lots of letter-writing took place. While you are at the Sterne-Hoya House, look at the book with replicas of letters Sam wrote to Anna. They are "cross-hatch" letters, meaning that they are written first in one direction on the page and then in another. This was done in order to put as many words as possible on each sheet of paper – a scarce commodity in those days.

Despite his courtship, in 1840 Anna married Dr. Robert Iron of Nacogdoches. Later that year, Houston married Margaret Lea in Marion, Alabama. As time went by, the Houstons had two children: a boy, Andrew; and a girl, Lea. While the Houstons lived in various places, their final home was in Huntsville, Texas.

We, along with every Texas history student in the state, know of Houston's military feats and political successes. But fewer know that when Sam Houston ran for governor of the State in 1859, the only campaign speech he made was from the steps of the "Nacogdoches University" building. In that speech he said, "Make primary education as free as possible, then build up your home colleges like the one we have here now."

Other lines in his address from the porch of Nacogdoches University include these that tell us something about his philosophy of education:

"…it is the duty of the legislature to provide for the education of the masses – not just your practical education, but the ABC's of private enterprise and philanthropy."

"…we have yet reached the point where we can afford to pay a tax to support an institution where only a favored few may be educated."

To working students he said, "that is the way to get an education – work for it… then...these colleges will not be full of pampered simpletons; but with men of the mind.

We Texans owe Sam Houston a great deal, and for many reasons, but chief among them are surely his leading the fight to free Texas from Mexico and pressing for the annexation of Texas to the United States.

OFFICERS OF RECONSTRUCTION

...a time for war and a time for peace...
Ecclesiastes 3

After the Civil War, U. S. soldiers were assigned to Nacogdoches for the duration of the Reconstruction Period (1865-1870). That was the period when states that had been in the Confederacy were required to make changes in their laws that would allow them to be readmitted to the Union. Federal officers and soldiers were placed in the state's cities to expedite the process while keeping the peace. Finding local space in our town for the officers to live and work was not easy, for they were, by the very nature of their work, unpopular new residents.

City leaders pondered where to put them. "What public buildings could the town release to them without making a hardship on local government? What space would the public most likely favor for their residence?" It was a puzzling and irritating issue to address – yet it had to be done. Finally, they decided on the Old University Building. That would mean delaying the resumption of education in the building, but it would place the soldiers and their officers in a fairly non-threatening place. – a few blocks away from downtown. With those deliberations, the decision was made. So for five or more years, the return of the building to its original purpose was delayed while The University Building was used as headquarters for the Nacogdoches Reconstruction Officers.

The U. S. soldiers and their officers took over the entire Nacogdoches University facilities, using some of the dormitory rooms and the spaces in the main building as well. However, there is some evidence that one of the small rooms in the lower part of the main building was reserved for a first grade classroom. As far as we know these unwelcome residents took reasonably good care of the building.

Their presence in town must have been somewhat irritating to the citizens but they were accepted with grace. One sad event remains as a major story in local folklore. Here's what happened:

For whatever reason – lack of refrigeration, or inadequate cooking, or any one of a number of other causes – there was an outbreak of dysentery among the officers. It was so severe that before it was brought under control, 21 of those U. S. soldiers died. "Where to bury them?" was a serious issue at the time. After much discussion, it was decided to bury them in the cemetery at Old North Church. There were already 47 Confederate veterans buried in that cemetery and it was located far out of town in a rural area not given to destruction of cemetery grounds. Old North Church was the oldest Protestant Church in the area - and the folks there were willing to have the soldiers buried in their grounds.

Today, we do not know where, in the cemetery, the grave is located. Local Folklore has it that the men were buried in a mass grave – OUTSIDE THE FENCE. Friends of Historic Nacogdoches, Inc. has (as one of its many goals,) a plan to use modern sensory technology to locate the graves and place an appropriate marker at the site.

SISTER JOSEPHINE

One sows and another reaps…
                                John 4

By 1870, the Civil War had ended and so had the reconstruction that followed it. Nacogdoches could, at last, reopen the University because the building was no longer needed to house the Confederate Hospital or the Reconstruction Offices. It could now return to its intended use as a place for higher education. Trustees of the University arranged for a Catholic Order to manage it for two years. Four nuns from Notre Dame were assigned as headmaster and teachers. They were Mother Superior, and Sisters Burnadette, Josephine, and Mary Paula. Their program focused on young students, but it was co-educational.

Sister Josephine was the one among the nuns whom the students loved – and she loved them. When the two-year school contract with the Catholics ended, Sisters Burnadette and Mary Paula choose to return to their home base, but Sister Josephine chose to remain in Nacogdoches. After her experience with the Nacogdoches University program of education, she felt that the children of local Spanish Families were being discriminated against. She sought ways she might alleviate this problem and she chose to begin with the Spanish families who owned large plantations in the Melrose area. She felt education was the key to reducing discrimination so she lived with the Spanish families, teaching their children, guiding them in community activities, and in their religious life.

When those children no longer needed her, she moved to the Moral community to teach their small school. She not only taught the school children, but she served as the religious leader in the community. In 1889, people in the Moral Community were able to build a new church and Sister Josephine moved into a small bare room at the back end of the building. There she lived, working with the children of the Moral families on week days and leading worship on Sundays. In general she ministered to the needs of the people by comforting the ill and dying, and attending to their many spiritual needs. They often had outdoor services during hot summer days. She led these services under a great black mulberry tree, called "El Moral."

In 1893, Sister Josephine fell ill. Her beloved congregation rushed her to a hospital in House where she died after a brief illness. For generations Spanish people in Nacogdoches have continued to tell stories of the love and care their families received from the "Sister from France."

In 1984, Sister Josephine was inducted into the Nacogdoches Hall of Fame.

STUDENT MEMORIES

...you shall know the truth and the truth will set you free...

John 8:32

In a time when only elementary education was available to children growing up in East Texas, our ancestors created Nacogdoches University in order to provide "higher education" for our young people. (At the time the high school movement had not reached the south. In fact it was only in 1822 that the first high school in the United States was created in Boston, Mass.)

Nacogdoches University operated as an institution of higher education until it (like all universities in the south) was closed for the duration of the Civil War. Soon after it was closed, it was converted to a hospital for Confederate soldiers.

After the war, the building was used for several years as offices for the Reconstructon Officers assigned to Nacogdoches. Around 1870, those offices were closed here and the building was returned to the trustees.

In this troubled time, the trustees decided to invite the Masons to run the school. At the time, the Mason's organizations were strongly focused on developing public schools in Texas. The Masons accepted only male students.

After the Masons completed their contractual period, nuns from the Catholic Church were invited to operate the school and they decided to open the school for young children as well as for older ones. Young ones were taught downstairs and older ones upstairs in the auditorium.

The trustees continued to be concerned with "higher education" so when the contact with the Catholics expired, the building was leased to Kechi College from Louisiana. They moved here in the 1880s and operated the school as a university for some years. However, at the end of their contact, trustees decided to again assume responsibility for the school and they determined to provide education for both young children and older ones. In effect they melded the program of "higher education" into Nacogdoches' first high school.

Here is a letter written by one of the students of the time – the late 1890s.

"I was a student at Nacogdoches University in the years following the Civil War. By that time, there were classes for young students as well as for upper level scholars. I boarded in Nacogdoches with Mr. and Mrs. Hale. My father (Dr. Sparks) brought me to their house every Monday morning and he came for me each Friday afternoon. I had a horse I loved to ride, so as a treat for me, he would bring my horse with him when he came on Friday and I was allowed to ride it home.

My classes were in the main building, although I had art and music in the dormitory. I also ate dinner with the girls and boys who lived in the dormitory. The dormitory was a frame building that sat just east of the University building. The boys and a male teacher lived upstairs in the dorm and the girls and a female teacher lived downstairs. Everyone ate together in the long dining room. After dinner, if we were thirsty, we had to go outside to the well and draw up a bucket of water to get a drink. And of course the toilet facilities were out back – somewhat north of the buildings.

I remember that when my boarding school friends wanted to go to town, they were only allowed to go if a teacher could go along to supervise their behavior and their shopping. A male teacher went with the boys and a female teacher accompanied the girls.

My mother worried about us students being in the building on really cold days. The building was heated by 12 fireplaces – even so, we were not comfortable on cold days. I heard my father say that it took a cord of wood a day to keep the place warm when there was a bad cold spell. The teachers usually stood near the fireplaces when they taught. But in front of each fireplace was a long bench and they allowed us students to take turns sitting on the benches. When we got good and warm, we went back to our desks and another group of students took our places on the bench in front of the fire.

…..such good memories!"-

Johnnie May Sparks Wyres (Letter in the Nacogdoches University Museum)

DR. BIRDWELL – FIRST DAYS AT SFASU

In the fall of 1923, the much-sought-after school, now known as Stephen F. Austin State University, opened as a "normal" school. That is, it was an institution whose purpose was to train teachers for the public schools of the state. Dr. A. W. Birdwell, a professor from Southwest Texas State Teachers College was chosen as the institution's first president. The 19 faculty members included names we see today on campus buildings and names we remember from long-term Nacogdoches residents. They include Wisely, teaching business, Hinds, agriculture, E. E. Davis, education, Mays, Spanish, Shelton, P. E., Garner, Social Science, Ferguson, Mathematics, Ida Pritchett, Music and Upton, Science.

There were 158 students enrolled for that first semester. Unfortunately, inclement weather delayed completion of the college's first building, so classes began that fall in shared space at Nacogdoches High school. Some met in the Old University Building, others in the Stone Fort (which was on the TJR campus at the time), and still others met in unused rooms of the high school building.

Many fascinating stories come from that time. In 2001, I interviewed the only two people who were still living who were in those first classes. One of them was Mr. Otis Floyd who told me this amusing tale.

In 1922, I was living with my parents and brother in Teneha, and I lacked one year finishing high school. My father was a carpenter, and when he learned about the large college building that was under construction in Nacogdoches, he moved us here where he was able to get a good job working on the building. Father was told that even though my brother and I had not finished high school, we could enter the college and finish high school in the "sub-college" program. (Courses somewhat like "dual-credit" courses of today.)

When I enrolled that first term, we learned that there were not enough students for the sub-college classes, but President Birdwell worked out a plan for us to take college level courses with the understanding that if our grades were good enough we would be awarded high school credit as well. In addition, we were allowed to test out of a course each in music, agriculture, and mathematics. In this way, we completed high school along with our first year of college.

Needless to say, such a program of study was extremely time consuming, and as you can understand, I looked for ways I could manage all those courses in the time I had. Now in those days, the year was divided into three "terms" rather than today's two "semesters." As we were registering for that first term, I. Heard that one could enroll in volleyball for the P. E. requirement and never have to attend class because there was not yet a volleyball court or a coach. Armed with that information, I enrolled. On the first day we were told that class meetings would be delayed pending a place to play. The person who met with the class told us that we would be notified when the court was ready. Well, we didn't hear from anybody all term and when grades came out, I had credit for P. E. That time saved had been a great help for me as I tried to complete all the courses required to reach my goals, so I decided to try the same thing again. And, again, the person who met the class announced a delay until a court was ready. And again, at the end of the term, we received credit even though the class had only had that initial meeting.

Now by the time the third term began, the college had moved into its building on the campus and when I enrolled for volleyball this time, a new coach had been hired and he called me into his office where he said, 'Mr. Floyd, I see you are an experienced volleyball student; I have here a rule book for volleyball and a ball and a net; I am assigning you to organize the other students who are enrolled and direct the classes!'

I asked, 'Mr. Floyd, what did you do!

"Well," he said, "I sat up all night studying that book of volleyball rules and when the class met, I chose the most athletic boy among the students to be the referee and the games began. We all learned how to play!"

He loved telling that tale and we laughed together at its happy ending.

Following a successful career as a teacher and school leader, Mr. Floyd had returned to Nacogdoches to live when he retired. He began teaching in a two-teacher school in a logging camp south of Lufkin. Soon he moved on to be an Ag teacher in Shelby County, then he served as a school principal, and finally taught math at a high school in Dallas.

An interesting side note: When Mr. Floyd got his first SFASU student ID card, he put it in his wallet and it stayed there for the remainder of his life. He often showed it with great pride.

DR. BIRDWELL AND THE FLOURNOYS

Dr. Birdwell would cross Texas to help a friend.

1930 SFASU Yearbook

Dr. A. W. Birdwell, Stephen F. Austin State University's first president, was a well-respected leader, much-loved by students and faculty. In 2001, I interviewed the two living students from that first semester in the fall of 1923, and they both wanted to tell me about Dr. Birdwell. Here is the story told by one of them: Mrs. Ruby Flournoy.

She came to SFA from a rural community that offered only an eighth grade education. However she longed to become a teacher and finally her parents agreed for her to move to Nacogdoches for training in the school for teachers. She enrolled in the "sub-college" program and spent a year student English, history, government, art, home economics and education. At the end of that year she was granted a "two-year, renewable" teacher's certificate and she left college to begin teaching.

During that first year, she met a handsome young man who was also teaching after just one year of college. They fell in love and vowing to their parents that they would find a way to return to college and get the longed-for degrees, they married. However, their teaching salaries didn't go as far as they had imagined, and at the end of that second year, when they were forced to return to college for summer classes or give up their teaching positions, they did not have money for the tuition and neither did their parents. What were they to do? They decided to go into Nacogdoches on registration day and seek a way to get into school without the required tuition. First they talked with the registrar seeking courses on credit. Of course, he could not enroll them, and they turned away in despair. Then they had an idea – perhaps Dr. Birdwell, the president, would help them.

They went to his office and he graciously invited them in to discuss their problem. They explained their situation, impressing him with their need to go to summer school if they were to be given contracts to teach in the fall. They had heard about scholarships, so they asked if there were scholarships at SFA. .

"Oh, no" he said, "the college had no scholarships at all!"

"But we must get into summer school or we will not be able to teach this fall!" they exclaimed.

"I'll tell you what I am willing to do." Dr. Birdwell said, "I'll take you downtown to my bank, introduce you to the loan officer and sign for you to get a loan."

And that's what they did. As they sat with the loan officer, Dr. Birdwell, asked, "How much do you need?"

"We have figured closely," they said, "and we think we can pay tuition and make it through the summer on $75.00."

Dr. Birdwell said, "Let's make it $90.00."

The loan enabled them to return to school during the summer term, then continue in their teaching positions in the fall. That year they saved a part of each month's salaries, repaying the loan before summer. For the next nine years they returned each summer to renew their teacher's certificates and work toward bachelor degrees. They graduated in 1934 and were awarded "life-time" teacher's certificates. They attribute their success as students and as life-long educators to Dr. Birdwell's wisdom and trust in SFA students.

PROFESSOR CAMPBELL

Achieve excellence without excuses.

E.J. Campbell

Professor E. J. Campbell was one of the best-known and most successful educators in the history of Nacogdoches Schools. During the years of segregation he was head of the "Colored" schools in Nacogdoches, and both races praised his leadership. They were thankful for his wise counsel and strong community presence. Armchair historians in our town say that the reason there has never been serious conflict between the races in Nacogdoches is due, in large part, to the influence of Professor Campbell and Dr. Nelson, beloved and much-respected local physician.

Professor Campbell's daughter, Willie Lee, often shared the story of her father's young life. He was born a generation after slavery, but at a time when segregation was a strong force in southern towns. He lived with his mother, father, and younger brother. They had a small farm that joined the plantation where his ancestors had been slaves. His father owned a fine horse – so much admired that he often had offers to buy it. Always he refused to sell. One day some white men came to the family home and asked Mr. Campbell if he would go with them to search for a missing neighborhood child. He readily agreed, saddling his horse and riding away with them. He was never seen or heard from again. Neither was his fine horse!

In a few months, Mrs. Campbell died, too, and the two boys were sent to live with various family members. E. J. lived first with their aunt and uncle who ran a fish camp on Angelina river and later with another aunt and uncle who lived in Garrsion near a school for colored children. There E. J. excelled, and when he finished the grammar school, the family made arrangements to send him to live with the pastor of a church in Nacogdoches because there was a high school here for colored students. Soon E. J. came to the attention of the local state representative who offered to send him to Prairie View A & M College for teacher training.

After a year in college he began teaching, and three years later, our town hired him to head the local schools for colored students. He was a master - at teaching math and at managing a school. He was excellent at public relations and at finding ways to solve problems in order to meet the growing needs of the school. For example, there was the problem of the school being on a red dirt road that was often impassable during the season of heavy rains. Professor Campbell made several requests for paving the roads, but the trustees were never able to address the need. Finally, one spring Professor Campbell invited the local Sate Representative to speak at Commencement. Then he prayed for rain.

AND his prayer was answered – in fact, during the week leading to the event, it rained every day, so much that the representative's car could only get as close to the school as East Main. He had to park the car on the roadside and walk on the muddy, rutted pathway from Main Street to the school. My, my, he arrived with muddy shoes, wet pants legs - almost breathless from the walk. At the next board meeting, trustees voted to pave the road to the school!

The curriculum, as well as the physical plant, was greatly improved, enriched with the addition of agriculture, home economics, shop, band, and football. Perhaps just as important was his plan to see more graduates go to college. Toward that goal, each May he took every student that would consider college, along with their parents, to spend a day at Prairie View College. They would gather at the Nacogdoches train station as early as four in the morning and spend the day at the college – an encouragement that eventually resulted in many college graduates from Nacogdoches.

Professor Campbell was also a loving, doting father to his only child. Willie Lee told this story that she called the "cake incident." It happened on a Saturday when Professor and Mrs. Campbell (as was their habit) went to their farm to work, leaving Willie Lee with the cleaning woman, Mrs. Mary Molandes. On these "Work Saturdays" Willie Lee always had chores – the main one being to bake a cake for the family. When the cake was all finished and cooled, Willie Lee would cut a big piece and wrap it for Mrs. Molandes to take home. On that particular Saturday, as they worked together, Mrs. Molandes mentioned that she had never had a whole cake. Willie Lee thought about that off and on all morning and when Mrs. Molandes was ready to go home; Willie Lee said "take this cake so your family will have some too!" Mrs. Molandes said, "Oh, no!" But Willie Lee insisted and finally the cake – the whole cake – went home for the Molandes family.

Later when Mrs. Campbell discovered there was no cake for their week end, she asked, "What made you give away ALL the cake?"

Willie Lee replied, "I just wanted them to have for once in their lives, what we have every week!" Mrs. Campbell was silent – no reply – a serious situation for little Willie Lee.

When Professor Campbell heard the story, he said, "It's all right little girl; I'll fix it." And with that, he stopped his work and drove into town to the local bakery and bought a cake to replace the one given away! Mrs. Glass spoke often about her father. She liked to share his philosophy with these sayings that he used often to guide her and others.

Selected items from Professor Campbell's Advice

- When you know, you care, and when you care, you share.
- Don't let a man give you advice on how to buy a saddle if he doesn't own a horse.
- Be on time; the game may be won in the first inning.
- Beauty is God expressing himself.
- Dream big dreams; then put on your work clothes.
- Save some of every dollar you earn.
- If you want to help someone, help him like himself better.
- A good man is too noble for anger; too courageous for doubt, and too full of God's love to hate
- Everyone can be good at something.
- Everyone is someone special; deal with every individual with respect!
- Leave nothing to chance; prepare yourself to perform with excellence.
- Take positive action, not defensive action.
- Never, never, never let yourself get into a fight.
- Prejudice is cancer of the soul.
- Life is too short to be little.
- Every new day is a chance to start over.
- When you give in to anger, you lose control.
- 'Savor life for all the love, kindness and happiness you can experience.

TEACHER, TEACHER!

*...When you leave this earth, you can take nothing
that you have received...only what you have given; a full heart
enriched by honest service, love, sacrifice and courage...*

St. Francis of Assisi

"Send them to me," she said, "send your students who cannot pass Freshman English to me. They will learn in my classes!" And they did! Her students learned because she convinced them that they could, and she showed them how to learn. Hundreds of students never forgot Mrs. Cecil.

When she was asked to help a specific student, she asked that the person be assigned to one of her classes, and when that happened she was committed to teaching and counseling them in ways that brought success.

She was extremely organized in both content and methods. She counseling with each student privately and asked them to commit to these practices:

1. Come to class every day
2. Begin all assignments as soon as they are made
3. Come for counseling after a low test grade or when more information about a specific concept is needed
4. Prepare for a test the day before it is to be, but don't sit up all night studying. Get out of bed a bit early and look over the major concepts to be tested; then go to class with confidence that you are prepared.

Never did she embarrass individuals in front of her class. Occasionally, she would mention a special event opportunity at the university because she promoted a balanced life of activities for the students. A co-worker remembered that Mrs. Cecil might just quietly make this remark in an informal discussion of teaching: "Nobody has taught until somebody has learned."

Her son, The Rev. Anthony Cecil, spoke of his mother and her teaching.

He said, "When I was in elementary school, I would sometimes find myself in mother's office in the Rusk Building after school. I was usually impatient to go eat at the Nance Café or play in Griffith Park. Invariable a student or two would drop by for counseling and because Mother never turned them away, I sat quietly, listening to the discussion between the two. Mother might be carefully explaining sentence diagrams; or when to use 'I' before e', or perhaps the difference between 'sit' and set,' 'its and 'it's,' 'lie' and 'lay,' 'led' and 'lead,' etc. My favorite rule, as I listened in on these conferences, was the way to determine when to double a terminal consonant before adding a suffix: 'a single consonant preceded by a single vowel should be doubled when the accent is on the last syllable or when the word is a single syllable. An example is the word, 'overrun,' which becomes 'overrunning' with the addition of 'ing.' A former student of hers will occasionally recite one of these rules to me and we laugh together about how she helped us learn English grammar."

He continued, "My mother and I would sometimes go on literary tours when I was older. We might visit the Browning Library in Waco, for example, or go to hear a descendant of the poet, lecture on 'My Last Duchess.' During longer vacation times, we might journey to Oxford to visit Faulkner's home, Rown Oak, or take a bus tour to Stoke Poges in England. Somehow my mother managed to work these little adventures into her teaching."

Mrs. Cecil lived life to the fullest. In retirement she led the way to the community's acceptance of the first assisted living facility in town. She made her choice of which apartment to buy and promptly engaged a decorator to furnish and accessorize her hew home. In a few years, when her son retired and moved back to Nacogdoches, she was able, with his help to visit many places she had not been able to visit in recent years. For example, one day she called a docent for the newly renovated historic building that was the home of the 1845 Nacogdoches University and arranged for a private tour. On the appointed day her son drove her to the building where she was welcomed by a docent who toured her through the lower level. When it was time to go to the upper level, her son asked, "Mother, can you climb these stairs?' "Certainly" she replied and so began the climb. They stopped on each 5th step to give her time to adjust her breating. Then on she went up, up, and up until she finally reached the second level. The docents were amazed at her delight in seeing the displays. "I had no idea you have such treasures here she exclaimed. As she paused at the display of 19th century costume, she quietly mused, "I wonder how my generation will be perceived one hundred years from now."

Finally she was finished upstairs and as the little group neared the stair way, she said quietly, "All the way up, I was thinking, 'I'll have to do down them, too!'" But with thoughts that the way down would be easier than the way up, she proceeded.

On the lower level, she marveled at the mementoes available for purchase. She made her selections and went away happy.

The docents waved her "good-bye" then spent the rest of the afternoon talking about this amazing 97 year old visitor!

Chapter V
Angels Sightings

AN ANGEL OF COLOR

*Thou are fairer than the children of men; full of
grace are they lips, because God has blessed thee forever.*

Psalms 45:3

They say a woman from Nacogdoches was an angel for the Texas schools just when one was most needed. Her name was Willie Lee Campbell Glass, the daughter of the well-respected and much loved head of the Colored Schools in our town during the first half of the last century. She was born into the segregated society that dominated society in the early part of the last century. Life was very different then than it is today. Neither of the great wars had been fought; the automobile was a new invention and electricity was found only in cities. Life was not easy for people in small towns of America, but for people of color, life was especially difficult. Slavery had been illegal for 45 years, but a well-defined system of segregation was firmly in place. For example, black people were not allowed to vote or buy land. Their schools were limited at best. In the

market places, social rules required them to wait in lines until all whites were served. There were separate entrances to public buildings, separate drinking fountains and separate restrooms. Hospitals, motels, and restaurants were for "whites only." Most work available to black people was manual labor with few opportunities for advancement. Their destiny
seemed to be lives of labor in the service of the white man.

Yet, Willie Lee picked up, not on the problems, but on their solutions. Guided by her parents' examples she broke all sorts of barriers – first black woman to get a master's degree at Iowa State University, youngest professor at Virginia State, and First Lady of Texas College. Still later, she was named as the first African-American consultant in the Texas Education System. This position allowed her to do great things to advance lives of Black people in the segregated society, and still later to guide hundreds of them through desegregation to successful living. At first when she traveled around the state she was not allowed to eat in restaurants nor stay in motels. Fortunately the white consultants came to her rescue over and over, allowing her to stay in their homes and homes of their friends as she traveled the state. School district by school district she worked with administrators until barriers were removed.

Both individuals and groups profited from her leadership. For example, at one point in early desegregation times, the head of Family Studies in the United States decided to include the black organization of young women in the national meeting. Many said it could not be done. Finally, this national leader asked Texas to allow Mrs. Glass to leader the delegation of black women. Mrs. Glass began immediately to prepare the young women in her delegation – they planned for appropriate dress, expected convention behavior, staying in hotels, eating in restaurants, working with people who are different. As a result the event was a success – a first after integration!

She remembered that once, at an early integrated conference, a conflict arose between the black young women and white young women. Mrs. Glass saved the day (and the convention) when she persuaded the black women to make a positive response rather than a defensive one. She had remembered her father's admonition, "Willie Lee, never, never, let yourself get into a fight."

Early in the advent of Head Start Programs in Texas, Mrs. Glass gave a large plot of her family's land in Nacogdoches as a location for the Head Start School Buildings.

Mrs. Glass continued her work to bring the races to live together peaceably until her sudden death at age 93. She never ceased to care for the needy, to raise the expectations of young people, and to prepare them for successful and satisfying living.

ANGELS AMONG US

...I was sick, and you visited me...

Matthew 7

Life was still segregated among workers in the South when a retired school teacher named Edna Johnson, went to work in a local factory. But change was coming, and as feared, there were soon whispers spread throughout the plant that two black women had been hired. The prevailing whispers carried the messages, "we'll just ignore them!"

The rumors were true for one Monday morning the two arrived for work. There was unusual quiet throughout the factory. When noon came, the two black women sat alone at a corner table in the cafeteria eating sack lunches they had brought from home. No one came near them.

Day after day, the pattern of that first day persisted. Finally, Miss Edna said to herself, "something must be done." And, with that thought in mind, the next morning, she packed a lunch for herself. When the lunch hour came, she took her lunch to the corner table and said to the women, "May I sit with you?" They graciously made room for her and as they ate, they chatted about families and work. Miss Edna continued eating with the two and in a few days she was able to recruit another woman from her car pool to sit at the expanding table. Eventually the women were accepted by a majority of the workers. Miss Edna became genuine friends with Lillian and Evelyn, as did many others in the plant.

It was just a year or two later that Miss Edna was diagnosed with an aggressive form of Leukemia with little hope of recovery. She was hospitalized in the city – a couple of hours away from her place of work.

One day as she lay quietly in her hospital bed with her husband and children nearby there was a soft knock at the door. Someone said, "Come in," and there entered a neat middle-aged black couple – strangers to the family. "Who could they be?" they wondered.

Then, in the blink of an eye, Miss Edna said, "OH, its Lillian!" and she reached out her arms as the beautiful black woman came to her bedside.

(It seemed that Lillian and her husband had each taken a vacation day from work and had driven the three hours to Dallas to visit their dying friend, the one who had befriended them when others would not.)

A BIG BLACK UMBRELLA

...the son of man will send his angels...
Matthew 13:41

It was a dark and stormy afternoon when I left work early to drive to my parents' home about three hours away. They were both ill and it was my turn to care for them through this week end. I was only a few miles into the trip when the rains began. I slowed the car, thinking the rain would soon cease, but it did not. In fact, the storm clouds gathered and as I drove along I could see downed trees and other evidence that there had been a tornado along this route very recently.

The storms continued all around me with increasingly heavy rains. Ditches alongside the roads were rapidly filling with gushing waters. Before I was aware of how severely the storms and rain were, I was in an area of deep ditches on each side of the two-lane roadway, with no place to turn off the road. As the rain became heavier, I could barely see the tail lights of the car in front of me.

No place to stop; waters rising; fear that a car behind me might crash into mine! It was so frightening! And it seemed I could do nothing but continue driving. I drove as slowly as I could, trying to keep in sight of the tail lights of the leading car. Those lights were the only sign I had that I was staying on the roadway!

As the waters threatened to wash over the entire highway, I determined to stop as soon as I could see a drive-way. "Perhaps I could spot a mailbox that would indicate a driveway or maybe a business near the highway," I thought. Nothing like that came into my sight and I became more frightened with each mile! Driving in the heavy rain was like swimming underwater with no option for surfacing!

Finally I saw a driveway and I turned onto it just hoping I was driving on solid ground. . "Maybe I could say in this place until the rain subsided," I reasoned. A loud clap of thunder, bright streaks of lightening, and drowning rain made me hunch into the seat of my little car.

Then a wonderful thing happened, for I had only sat there a minute or two when I realized someone was knocking on the car window. Through the rain I could dimly see a man with a big black umbrella standing at the car window. I lowered it and he said, "Mam, you have reached a used car lot with a small building just steps away. Come in and be safe until this storm subsides." As a loud burst of thunder sounded, and a streak of lightening flashed right in front of the car, I decided his offer was my best bet for survival.

He held the umbrella over us both as I got out of my car and walked with him to the little office building. Two other men were there and they asked, "What are you doing out in this storm." I explained and the one with the umbrella said, "Use our phone and call your parents; tell them where you are – that you are safe, and that you will continue when the storm passes. "

That is what I did and in due time I was on my way, but ever after when I think of angels, one of them is carrying a BIG BLACK UMBRELLA.

AN ANGEL IN A WHITE COAT

I was sick and you came to me...
Matt. 25:35

An elderly farmer named Smith lived in a small village in North East Texas and in his own words, he seldom, if ever, found a need to go outside his home county. However, that changed when he was struck with a sudden and serious ailment. Local doctors said he needed a specialist for an operation. They were pleased to get him into the care of a noted surgeon, Dr. Jones at Baylor Hospital in Dallas.

As soon as possible the family made the trip to Dallas to see the specialist. When Mr. and Mrs. Smith met him they liked the doctor right way. He was knowledgeable, sophisticated and confident, but he was also kind and compassionate. After an examination, he said, "Yes, I will take your case, but before we can consider surgery, we must get control of this infection. We'll get you into the hospital right away and start the treatment immediately."

With each of the waiting days that followed, Mr. Smith became more and more frightened and anxious about the surgery to come. His anxiety increased when he discovered that by an unbelievable coincidence, his operation was scheduled to take place in an operating room where his own father had died during a surgical procedure 25 years earlier. Finally, the apprehensive became so pronounced it threatened to derail the entire treatment. The family asked for increased medication but the doctor was reluctant. He said to Mrs. Smith, "I'm going to try something else that may work," and with that he went into the hospital room and said "Mr. Smith, you and I are going to take a little tour today; I want to explain to you the equipment we have in the operation theater and show you how your surgery will be done."

In an hour or so, Mr. Smith was back in his room, saying to his family, "you won't believe what all they have there - not only to do normal procedures - but to actually keep a person from dying. Why, I don't think it would be possible for a person could die in that room!"

With that assurance, the surgery soon took place and recovery was swift. And as the days passed, the country farmer and the city doctor seemed to gain more and more appreciation for each other, until, when the day came to check out of the hospital, Mr. Smith said, "Come to us one day this fall and I'll take you squirrel hunting." "Set the date!" responded the doctor.

They agreed on the first day of the hunting season.

Later, on the appointed day, Dr. Jones drove a couple of hours across the state on the new interstate highway, then turning off it, he drove slowly through a small town named Cumby, then onto a narrow road to a little community near the creek that ran through a thick woods. In the center of that village he found the Smith home. If he were bothered by an ancient farm house, or by going to the barn for the night chores, or by multiple evidences of the difference between city and country, he did not show it. Perhaps the differences were made tolerable by the late dinner Mrs. Smith served: fried ham, hot biscuits with brown gravy, mashed potatoes, butterbeans, and fresh turnip greens. Of course the main course was followed by coconut meringue pie and all was served with tall glasses of iced tea.

Up early the next day the men had a long and successful hunt. That evening, the main course was luscious fried squirrel! As the doctor left, he asked if he might bring his teenage son for a hunt later in the season. "Of course,' the family said, "you will be welcome!"

In a couple of weeks the doctor, with the 14 year old son in tow, came again. The young teenager, directly from Dallas's prestigious Highland Park Community, helped milk the cows, gather the eggs, and feed the pigs. But, as planned, the squirrel hunt was the main event. The doctor chose to spend his morning reading under the big shade tree while the man and boy went hunting. Early in the morning, they went into the woods where all quiet except for the chirping of the birds. They came with soft steps and spoke not a word. Watching the high branches of the trees as they walked along, the boy tapped the man's shoulder and pointed to a squirrel climbing high in a tall oak. The man motioned the boy to sit on a nearby stump and get his gun ready. The man approached the tree and as he did the squirrel spotted him. The man slowly began to circle the tree. As he moved clockwise around the tree, the squirrel also moved, keeping the tree trunk between him and the man. But the squirrel did not see the boy with the gun. The man circled slowly, and just when the squirrel moved into a position where the boy could sight him, he fired the gun. The squirrel dropped to the ground dead. "Good shot! Said the old man, "Let's move on 'til we see another one, and we'll try that again." The two were "still-hunting," that is, they were hunting without a dog but even so they got a good number of squirrels. The old man preferred to hunt alone, but today was different – he owed a big favor!

Home with the squirrels the man cleaned each one. He cut a gash at the base of the long bushy tail; then he made cuts around the upper part of each leg. Next, putting his foot firmly on the bushy tail, and using both hands, he pulled the skin from the back end of the squirrel to the head – sort of turned it wrong side out. With a sharp knife he cut off the head and gutted the body.

"Let me try one," said the boy and after a few trials he would be able to go home with a brand new skill. After a couple of washes at the outside water faucet, the squirrels were ready to take inside to the kitchen. Mrs. Smith fried them for their noon time meal. While they slowly cooked, she made biscuits. When the squirrel was done, she makes creamy, flavorful gravy and when the biscuits were baked, they all sat down to a fine meal. The big goblets of iced tea that accompanied it and the apple pie that followed made for good eating!

A few weeks later, the Smiths returned to Dallas for a final check-up. When the examination and consultation were over, Dr. Jones stood and came around the desk with hand out-stretched. "Mr. Smith," he said, "I am dismissing you as my patient, but I'd like to keep you as my friend."

"Sir," came the reply, "you and your family will always be welcome in our home." And so it was that their friendship continued for years to come!

Angels in action!

ANGELS IN THE JURY BOX

...I was in prison and you came to me...
　　　　　　　　　　　　　　　Matthew 25

The jury had been given their charge, and the twelve people withdrew to decide on a guilty or not guilty verdict. Guilty, that is, of murder!

The accused was a teenager, though old enough to be tried as an adult. He was charged with murder in the first degree because of the death of another teen with whom he had been fighting. In retrospect, I suppose it was a predictable encounter. It happened on a Saturday night when a group of young people were milling around the town center, visiting, smoking, and looking for dates if they had not already found one.

The two who began the fight represented polar opposites – one from the country - the other from town; one an athlete - the other a musician; one a farmer's son - the other a doctor's son; one big and burly - the other small and thin. But, both of them were interested in the same girl.

What triggered the fight? No one knows for sure – it simply began and of course the biggest one looked to win. In desperation the smaller one reached into his pickup to get something to use for hitting the other fellow. He came up with a file, and as he flung it toward the other one, it sank into the big fellow's chest - just in the place to be fatal.

The families, the community, were all devastated! How could this have happened? What a tragedy! Of course, the teen was charged and as the court day neared, the family mortgaged their farm to pay for the best attorney they could find.

There was, of course, no question of the killing, but there was a big question about what to do with the guilty teen.

After the prosecuting lawyer summed the event and asked for a guilty verdict with life imprisonment, the defending lawyer took the stand. With the eloquence of a wise and experienced counselor he made these points.

"Ladies and gentlemen of the jury," he began, "we have lost one of our finest young men in this tragic event, and now you must decide whether or not we will lose the second one!"

"We agree completely with the belief that this event should not have taken place, but we hold firmly to the belief that neither young man planned to kill the other. In fact, some fighting is not an uncommon activity among young people, and but this one went terribly, terribly wrong through no malice of forethought. I urge you to give this boy left among us the opportunity to finish growing up, to live the good life that we want for all our children. Certainly you can send him to prison for life, but what will that accomplish?"

"Through the ages, many people have had this hard decision to make when young people make wrong choices. For example, the greatest man in the Old Testament, Moses, had a similar event in his life. Have you ever thought what would have happened to civilization if Moses had been put in prison for life because he killed a man? "

"Well, first, the greatest horde of slaves ever known would not have been freed. Further, the greatest code of ethic, The Ten Commandments, would not have been written, and the first organization of representative government would not have been created."

"But these things did happen because Moses was given a second chance."

"That's what I ask you to do for this young man. Send him home with his parents, give him a chance to finish growing up. Let him seek forgiveness and begin a life of service and productivity."

"When you do that, we will have truly found justice with mercy with and hope for the future of the world which will ultimately be entrusted to this generation of young people."

The jury did, in fact, choose a ruling that allowed the young man to go free. That was some years ago, and people who have followed the case, continued to stand amazed at the productive life the young man has lived – business man, minister, community servant.

All this because there were, no doubt, angels in the jury box!

A WHOLE FLOCK OF ANGELS

Be doers of the word, and not hearers only.
James 1:22

One day recently as a young lawyer left his office building for lunch, he was startled to see someone lying under a tree at the edge of his property. Going closer he discovered it was a young teenage boy asleep in the shade. A backpack and a puppy on a leash were nearby. Leaning down he gently shook the boy's shoulder, and the young fellow waked immediately. The lawyer asked if he were in need of help. As the boy explained his situation, the lawyer invited him into the office where some of his staff offered him food and drink. As he ate, they fed and watered the dog. When he finished eating, the seemingly well-mannered and friendly boy told this story.

He had left his home in Oregon with his father, and his father's girlfriend, driving to Florida on vacation. On one of their gas stops the boy encountered a stray dog. The two made friends and the father allowed him to take the dog with them.

A few days into the trip, they began to experience problems. First, there was car trouble; then his dad stopped at a casino and lost most of their money. To make matter worse, the father began drinking and the more he drank, the angrier he became. He was belligerent with both the boy and the girlfriend. Finally they stopped to sleep (in the car) at a Pilot Truck Stop just outside the town. Very early in the morning, the boy waked to hear and see his father shouting and hitting at the girl friend. The two had been fighting and arguing the day before, and now it was beginning again. As the blows grew worse for the woman, the young man tried to intervene. That angered the father who turned on the son, striking out at him as well. As his anger intensified, the man jumped from the car, ran around to the back door of the car and, reaching in, and dragged the boy with his backpack and his dog onto the street. Then the father hopped into the car and sped away, leaving the boy on the roadside.

"What to do?" He had been sleeping without shirt or shoes and if he were to walk very far, he needed at least something for his feet. Finally he decided he would walk until he came into town, and if there were a Wal-Mart, he would hang out in its parking lot until he could beg shoppers for enough money to buy shoes and a shirt. With that decision, he began walking toward lights he saw in the distance.

He had not walked far when a policeman saw the boy and pulled over to question him. When he heard his story he gave him a ride to Wal-Mart. Parking the car, the policeman went into the store with the young man and bought a pair of shoes, two shirts, and some underwear for him. As the boy was in a dressing room putting on the new clothing, the policeman explained the situation to the Wall Mart clerk. She was so moved by the boy's plight that she gave the policemen a discount on the clothing and when the boy came from the dressing room, she tucked something in his pocket and said, "Take this and go get yourself some breakfast,."

The policeman drove the boy to a community-help center and left him sitting outside the building waiting for it to open. By this time, the boy said he simply wanted to go home; he had an aunt and a grandmother back in Oregon who would take him in. When the agency opened, people there said they could probably help him, but first they must do some checking. He was told to come back later in the day. As he went outdoors he noticed a large tree in the lot next door and he thought to rest awhile in its shade.

Now the agency happens to be located next door to the law office and that is where the lawyer had earlier found him sleeping.

After hearing his story the law office secretary called the bus station for information about a time and ticket for a return to Oregon. She was dismayed to discover that the last bus of the day had already left. The boy said, "Not to worry; I'll just sleep in the parking lot and get a bus tomorrow." "Oh no," the lawyer said, "I will drive you to the bus station in Dallas (70 miles away) and you can get the bus to Oregon from there."

Off they went, making a quick stop at the bank for the lawyer to get some cash for the boy so he would have money to get from the station to his aunt's home. As they sped along to meet the bus leaving Dallas, the boy and his dog fell asleep with the dog snoring all the way.

When they arrived at the station, they were told that the company would not allow dogs on the bus. To the boy, the lawyer said, "We have a problem, buddy," What do you want to do?" The boy looked at his puppy, then at his benefactor and said, "Sir, everything I have is what's in this backpack, and this dog. I really want to keep him with me if I can."

Perplexed at the problems they were encountering, the lawyer asked, "Well, have you ever flown in an airplane?"

"No sir, but I would be willing to."

With that answer they made a late day dash across Dallas to Love Field Airport. At the ticket counter they learned they could take the dog but it must be in a crate. Away they went to the nearest pet shop; bought a crate; and hurried back to get the last plane of the day to Oregon. The lawyer explained to the ticket agent that he was helping a young boy get home and the compassionate fellow gave them a discount on the ticket.

At security the young lawyer and the young boy said goodbye, shook hands and soon the boy was on his way to Portland, Oregon, with money in his pocket to get a taxi to his aunt's house.

A late night call from Oregon confirmed his safe arrival. He was at his aunt's and she was happy to have him. In a few days, a Facebook message brought more thanks to the lawyer and assurance that the boy was doing well with care from aunt and grandmother!

The police officer, the Wal-Mart clerk, the community organization people, the law office secretary, Southwest Airlines, and the young lawyer – what a flock of angels!

THE TIRED MULE

...better is a neighbor who is near than a brother who is far away...
Prov. 27:10

In the small village of our childhood, the store porch was the source of all community information and the place where most decisions that affected the general welfare were made. Busy farmers stopped by early in the morning to get whatever supplies they needed for working the land. Old men came throughout the day to sit, share information and speculate on the future, while the younger men came after the workday ended to have a coke and visit with their friends. As a group they shared information more accurate and more thorough than a daily newspaper would have – if they had had one. In the late winter, early spring, and summer, vegetable gardening was likely to be the most frequent topic discussed among the men. The garden, of course, was critical to the family's food supply and the earlier its products ripened the better the family ate.

Our father took great pride in his garden. His work there began in February when he turned the soil with the biggest of his plows. Then after pulling the "harrow" over the whole garden to break up the big clumps of soil, the rows were made and planting began. Usually the first planting was of potatoes – these must surely be in the ground by Valentine's Day! While most farmers had tractors for this gardening, our father used the old fashion method of horse-drawn plows. He and his horse, Snip, had been gardening partners for 27 years and he preferred that old method.

Throughout the season the garden was an important topic on the store porch. Early in May one might say to another, "Did I hear you had new potatoes at the dinner-on-the ground Saturday?"

"Well, yes," replied our father, "my old Pappy always tried for that and the women expect it." Modestly, he continued, "Sometimes, of course, the weather won't cooperate, but I was lucky with it this year."

Another might say, "The way the corn is growing I'm expecting to gather our first mess of roos-nears soon."

"My, that is early," exclaimed another.

Sitting quietly nearby was a newcomer – a city boy who had married a local girl and they had come home to visit her grandparents.

"Roos-nears?" he queried. "What are they?"

Most of the men lowered the heads, quietly shaking them at such ignorance. One decided to explain. "In the early days, corn was the main crop and as soon as the first little ears appeared they were pulled and roasted in the shuck over the outdoor cooking fire. Somehow that term "roasting ears" has come to sound like "roos-nears." "They are mighty good the way my wife cooks them." And immediately the conversation turned to the various ways of cooking this common delicacy.

One day a stranger - a man of color from small community in the next county – came to the store, and as he sat with the men on the porch he told the story that has come to be called the story of The Tired Mule.

"I was hired," he began, "by the sons of that old man that lives across the road. They say he's near 90, spent a lot of the winter in the hospital, and is still determined to make a garden. His old horse died last year and he don't have no way a'tal to break the soil. Somebody told them boys, who don't live around here anymore, about my mule and plow, and last Saturday they come to my house and asked if I would help their father make a garden the old timey way. That's what I have been doing today, but I don't mind telling you, I am glad it is over. When I got there a little after daylight, the old man was sitting out under that big tree with his seeds and cabbage plants and onion plants all ready to put in. He told me to go first with the mule and plow and make the rows, and then he would follow me, dropping in the seeds and little plants. Well, sir, as the morning wore on I thought the old fellow would surely drop dead! He stumbled, tottering amongst the rows, slow as a snail, but still he insisted on going on. Finally I told him I was tard, and that my mule was really tard. I asked if we could go up to the house and sit under the shade tree to rest for just a little while. He agreed. I decided if I could get him to the tree I would not let him back in that garden – I sure didn't want him dying on my watch! After we drank a couple of glasses of ice tea, he said, 'let's get back to work'. I had to think fast.

"Sir," I said, my mule is just too tard to work anymore. I wonder if you would stay here under this good shade and hold the bridle so he won't stray while I go back and finish the planting. - "Yes, sir," I emphasized, 'My Mule is sure Tard.'" And the old fellow agreed. "Man! Was I relieved!"

With that division of labor the old man's last garden was finally planted! Could any angel have excelled that gracious man with his mule and plow!

HOLY CATS

...train up a child in the way he should go and he will not depart from it...

Proverbs 22

Down on the farm it had been a hot summer. But the cotton was all "laid by" - waiting now for it to mature enough to be picked. The women had almost finished the canning and drying of food for the winter, and the men were gearing up for the harvest. It was just the right time for the "Protracted Meeting." That is, it was time for the annual series of sermons that involved everyone in the community. The Presbyterians joined with the Methodists and choosing a fine preacher from afar, they organized the sermons to be preached (along with fine singing) every evening for two weeks. Everybody in the community attended.

At the end of the two weeks, on a hot Sunday afternoon, all those who had made a commitment to Christ gathered, along with their friends and family, to be baptized in the nearest creek. This year there was a goodly number and it was a particularly fine service. Even the little children were quiet and still as the holy service began. Each person was immersed in the cool, clear water as the preacher repeated: "I baptise you in the name of the Father, Son, and Holy Ghost."

Finally, it was over and families made haste to get home and get ready for a week of farm work. Now one of the young families was the Burns family who had a new baby. She joined two brothers, one a toddler and one about four years old. Early Monday morning, after Mr. Burns had left for the fields, Mrs. Burns was busy nursing the baby, cooking the noonday meal, and sorting clothes out for washing. About mid-morning she put the baby down to sleep and went outdoors to check on the boys who were playing in the front yard.

At least they were supposed to be playing in the front yard under the shade tree – each had strict instructions to stay there where their mother could see them as she checked on them regularly.

But alas, they were nowhere to be seen. She looked out every window, called from the front yard, the back yard – even went up to the roadway on the off chance they had gone for the mail. Despite all this, she could not find them. Where could they be; as she pondered that question, she remembered that the barn cat had recently had a litter of kittens. Perhaps, she thought, they were playing in the corn crib with the cats. She rushed to the barn, but there were no signs of cats or boys.

Her worries mounted!

As she rushed back to the house to check on the baby, she rounded the corner of an outhouse where they kept their barrels of water - spring water for drinking and cooking and pool water for cleaning and watering the animals. What a sight she saw! The boys had pushed an empty short barrel up to the barrel of spring water and turned it upside down so they could stand on it. As she watched, the toddler handed a kitten to the 4-year old who said (as he dipped the cat in the drinking water), "I baptize you in the name of the Father, Son, and Holy Ghost!'

The mother was paralyzed with the sight – ruined was all the drinking water – her husband would have to make a trip with the horses and sled to get another barrel before night!

"Oh, no!" she said, "Oh, no!"

As she pondered the situation, she heard the last of the "I baptize you's…" and, wiping her teary eye on her apron, she headed to the house saying aloud, "Well, at least we have holy cats, and just maybe a preacher in the making!"

A BARBED WIRE FIX

...I was a strange and you took me in...
Matthew 7

Sometimes angels are moving about in the dark of night – unrecognizable until someone needs their help.

I watched one of those angels at work during a cold winter night in 1955. Actually I was riding in the backseat of the car that was driven by the yet undiscovered angel. I had been with him and his wife taking a vacationing soldier to the bus station in Dallas so that he could return to his post in El Paso after the Christmas vacation.

It was a cold, cold night; the bus was late; and so it was after midnight when we left the station to return to our home about two hours away. The streets leading out of the city were quiet – very few cars about as the clouds above us threatened rain and sleet.

When our car came to a street light near the northeastern edge of Dallas, the car that was stopped in front of us did not move when the light turned green. We waited while the light turned red again and green again, and still the car remained, unmoving. Our driver decided to get out and see if there were a problem in the stalled car.

Indeed there was! In fact, when he returned, he told us that the car in front was being driven by soldier who was on his way home to Mississippi on leave and neither he nor the young soldier knew what to do to get the car started. With no other option for helping the young man, he decided to push the stalled car to the nearest gas station where he could surely get help.

Slowly the bumpers of the two cars connected and the push began. On and on we went – at a snail's pace, of course – thinking to find a service station that was open. What a deluted idea! We reached the far edge of Dallas without finding a single one. The men stopped the cars and talked again. They decided that our driver would continue to push the ailing car on to the next small town and get help there. They reasoned that there would surely be a night-watchman who could call a local mechanic to come out to help a soldier who was stalled on his way home.

However, when we found the night watch-man, who was circling the town square, he said the town's only mechanic was away for the week!

Back to the pushing.

Out on the highway, our driver realized that even his good car would not last long pushing the soldier's car. He must find another way. Finally, he stopped by the side of the highway, and taking his wire clippers from the tool box in the trunk of his car, he walked down a steep sloop and through a ditch of water, to a barbed wire fence surrounding a field of grain. With his car lights shining on the fence, he snipped out a strand of wire about 20 or 30 feet long. With it, he tied the front bumper of the soldier's car to the back bumper of our car , thinking that his motor might pull the car whereas it wouldn't last long pushing another car. He explained, "We'll pull him to Greenville and leave the car at a shop there where I know the mechanic. I can leave a note and he will fix the car as soon as the shop opens."

He paused, looking down with a bothered expression, he said, "I know the Lord will forgive us for this theft of wire; and I think the farmer would, too, if he knew the situation."

With our car pulling the soldier's car, we did, indeed, get the bum car to a shop in Greenville about three o'clock in the morning. Then, with the soldier in our car, we sped on home to Commerce.

The next morning the lady fed the young man a big breakfast – eggs, bacon, toast, homemade jam, coffee and orange juice. Then she made a packet of food for him in anticipation of his needs on the remainder of his trip. Around noon, our driver took the young man to the repair shop; paid the repair costs; and the soldier was finally on his way home!

Angels among us!

Chapter VI

First Folks, Nacogdoches

NACOGDOCHES, CELEBRATING 300 YEARS!

As the Tricentennial celebrations began, many people wanted to know how the date for the beginning of Nacogdoches was set. Local historians James Partin, Joe and Carolyn Ericson and Archie McDonald, explained it this way in their 1995 book, *NACOGDOCHES, The History of Texas' Oldest City*.

"Nacogdoches began as a Caddo village and is named for these first citizens. Since 1716 a succession of Spaniards, Anglo-Celts, and African Americans have occupied the area continuously."

The writers continued with information that explains how the beginning date for the founding of Nacogdoches was determined. At the time, the territory was owned by Spain; however, France was making various attempts to invade the area. Their activities prompted Spain to make a decision to establish missions in various parts of Texas, especially in East Texas. The Spanish governor of this territory recommended the establishment of a line of four forts from Coahuila, Mexico to the land of the Tejas Indians in East Texas. This, he thought, would prevent further foreign intrusions and insure peaceful conversion (to Christianity) of the Indians. However, the Fransciscan Priest, Father Massanet, who was part of the expedition to Texas, recommended seven missions, and that is the plan that was chosen. In January 1691, a newly appointed governor of Texas and Father Massanet began an expedition to East Texas with a plan for establishing the missions; however, for multiple reasons, their attempts failed.

Some years later a man named Captain Ramon led a group that did reach the Spanish goal of missions in East Texas. And included among them was the one that marked the beginning of the town of Nacogdoches. Partin and others explained: *Captain Ramon traveled about nine leagues east-southeast of Mission Concepcion (near Goodman Bridge) to the Nacogdoche village on the site of the present city of Nacogdoches. There he founded a third mission, Nuestra Senora de Guadalupe de los Nacogdoches. On July 9, 1716, after erecting a temporary log church and dwelling houses for the missionaries, he gave possession of the mission to Father Antonio Margil de Jesus...The mission stood on a slight rise overlooking Banita Creek. The establishment of this mission marked the first formal occupation by Europeans of the site of the present city of Nacogdoches.*

Thus, this year, 2016, Nacogdoches citizens celebrate the town's tricentennial – 300 years of living in a beautiful part of the world. The city, the chamber, businesses, the schools, social organizations, individuals and groups, found all manner of ways to celebrate this "once ever" time.

At the old University Building-the 300th anniversary was celebrated with a exhibit showcasing groups of people who have made their homes in Nacogdoches. The following pages are written as if from the diaries of young women whose families made Nacogdoches their home.

A PAGE FROM A YOUNG INDIAN GIRL'S DIARY

Our people in the piney woods have had many foreign invaders over the years and most resulted in bloodshed. But now new types of people have come – men in strange robes telling us of a God unlike any our people have known. Soldiers came with the men and they built something in our village that they call a "mission." They demand we work as they wish and obey them. Our people do not like this.

The missionaries have been bothered by our dress, thinking we made ourselves 'hideous' because of our custom of making our heads elongated. They did not like our body markings (tattoos). My mother did my body markings using a sharp stone to prick my skin. Next she rubbed on powdered charcoal, and when it healed my face was streaked from forehead to nose and tip of chin. We also paint our bodies for special occasions. I have a collection of pretty shells, bones, feathers, and stones to wear in my ears nose and hair. Sometimes I wear them as a necklace or on my wrists. My special dress is a tanned deerskin. We use deer and buffalo brains to turn our leather into a lustrous black color. My best dress is fringed and decorated with small white seeds. Of course I wear moccasins in winter and under my dress, I wear a breechclout which is made of grass or straw.

We produce all the food we need. Our men and women work to plant corn, beans, squash, sunflower seeds and tobacco. Men do the heavy work but we all work. Our main tools are hoes. After we gather our food, we burn off each field where it grew. Our meat comes from deer, buffalo, and bears. We render the fatty bear meat and store it in jars for the winter. Of course we also eat small animals like birds and fish wild hogs, prairie chickens, turkeys, mice and snakes.

We work together as a community. When my brother and his family needed a new house, the entire village came for a "house-raising." Of course my brother and his wife prepared a feast for the workers after they finished.

Our bows are made of wood from the Bois d'arc or Osage Orange trees. We use gourds to make rattles and flutes are made from bird bones and hollow reeds. I play the flute and my parents like that very much.

We make a varied of pottery. We also make all sorts of reed baskets and mats. Even though we have in our village all we need, we do trade with people who occasionally come from the west. We often trade the bow wood and salt to them for pretty green stones and warm blankets.

(Written by Ms. Virginia Alders, printed with Mrs. Alder's permission)

A PAGE FROM A YOUNG SPANISH GIRL'S DIARY

My name is Maria Veralda Arriola; I was born in a village near the Presidio San Antonio de Bejar in 1771. My father, Marcelino de Arriola was a brave Spanish soldier. In 1768 he brought my mother, Juana Maria Palacios, and my two older siblings to these new lands of the Tejas. He was with the presidio San Antonio de Valero, later called the Alamo. I am the youngest of four. My brother, Ascensio, and I were baptized in the parish church of San Fernanado.

My father was killed by Indians while he was patrolling along the Rio Colorado. After that, my mother decided to join the Adaesanos led by Captitan Gil Y'Barbo, who was planning to move back to their homes in Nacogdoches. The journey to Nacogdoches was long but in the spring of 1779, we arrived at the abandoned mission, Mission Nuestra Senora de Guadalupe. I was awed by the majestic trees, abundance of wild game, the hills and the streams. The lands were the most beautiful I had ever seen. We settled north of the Royal Highway, El Camino Real, where it crossed the LaNana Creek. We were near the central plaza and Y'Barbo's Stone trading center.

There was a beautiful place on ou land called Los Ojos de Padre Margil. This was the holy place where in 1718 Padre Antonio Margil de Jesus struck a stone and brought forth a continuous gush of water for the Indians during a severe drought. We spent many hours there playing in the cool springs and listening to stories about the miracle of Padre Margil.

Our daily life was regimented as we carried on the customs and culture of our European ancestors. We rose before dawn to pray. Afterwards we worked in the vegetable gardens of beans, corn and peppers. We gathered acorns, nuts and berries for the harsh winters ahead. These we ground in wooden bowls with a rock pestle. My brothers hunted in the nearby forests for deer, rabbits, bear, coyotes, and fish.

The church bells were important parts of our lives. We could hear them clearly and they were the priest's way of communicating with all our people. In the evenings they called us to prayer with a steady toll.

In 1792, a representative of the King of Spain came to our home and he and my motheWe gathered for Mass in the church near the Stone House, and prayed for our deceased loved ones, and to thank God for bringing us safely to our new home.

One day Jose Cayetano da Zepeda, a representative of the King of Spain, came to our home and walked our fields with my mother. He took note of the work that we had done. He led my mother to each corner of our large league of land, and in a sign of possession she drove stakes, pulling up grass and threw stones. She was the only woman in our pueblo to have this honor. This was the 4th day of May 1792, and the glorisou day I vowed to carry on her legacy as a strong Spanish woman.

(Written by Mrs. Peggy Jasso and printed here with her permissin)

A PAGE FROM A YOUNG ANGLO GIRL'S DIARY

My name is Jane Johnson and I came to Texas with my family in 1836, the year Texas became an independent nation. My father is a Circuit Rider and he was assigned as a missionary to Texas. Papa was born in North Carolina and Mother was from the Louisiana DeMoss family – French people. We live in a small community in East Texas. My older brothers do the farm work while Pape is away. We girls help Mama cook, sew, clean and do yard work.

Our house is a log house with four rooms; the front room, the back bedroom, and the upstairs room where the boys sleep. Our kitchen is just a few steps from the back of the house. Father made a dresser, bed, and dining table for our home during the first winter we were here. Of course we have some straight chairs and one rocker. Two big chests hold our bedding and out of season clothing. Each bedroom has convenient hooks for hanging the clothes we wear daily. We walk to the local community school that is less than 2 miles from our house. Mother is teaching me to sew. I already have two work dresses and with the new one I am making I will have two Sunday dresses. When I work in the garden I wish I could wear pants like my brothers, but of course no girl would dare to dress in pants!

My favorite food is friend chicken; my brothers prefer our cured pork. We eat vegetables from our garden all year. Fresh vegetables are available in spring and summer and the root vegetables are available from our cellar in the winter.

We walk to church every Sunday – the service is in the school house, so it's not far away.

(Written by Patsy Hallman, based on the life of her Great-great grandmother.)

A PAGE FROM A YOUNG AFRICAN-AMERICAN GIRL'S DIARY

My name is Evie and I came to Texas in the early 1880s when I was working as a cook for the president of Kechi College in Louisiana. Leaders of that college decided to move to Texas where they contracted to house their program in the Nacogdoches University building. The president brought all his staff. We have rooms in the dormitory building that is between the main building and Mound Street. I don't have much education, but I can read and write because President DeMoss allows us kitchen and grounds workers to go to Sunday afternoon worship services and reading classes that are held in a little school building near the creek. In the summer there is a reading class taught there as well.

Last week when I went to church I met the most handsome young man. His name is Lawson Reed and he has a good-paying job working on the railroad. Nacogdoches is building its first railroad and lots of colored men work on it. Of course that is hard work and dangerous, too. A couple of weeks ago one man fell while carrying a bucket of hot tar. Because there is no hospital here for coloreds, folks just took him home. We are all praying that he lives through it.

I dream of having my own family. In my dreams, Mr. Reed asks me to marry him and we make our own family. He is a good man; he preaches on Sundays. I can imagine that we would build a house near the church (it would have an extra room to take in young people from the country who want to go to high school – we might even have a room for the doctor to use for his really sick folks!)

(Editor's note: Evie did marry Mr. Reed and they spent a lifetime helping individuals and the community. Their descendants are fine people found throughout the community. This diary page was created by Patsy Hallman from OUB files and interviews with Mr. McMichael, long time educator and administrator in Nacogdoches schools.)

A PAGE FROM A YOUNG MEXICAN-AMERICAN GIRL'S DIARY

I came to Nacogdoches when I was 14 – came over the Texas border with my sister who was already living in Texas. I came because there were so many at home (9 brothers and sisters) and I wanted to find a place where I could work and have a good life.

Soon after we got to Nacogdoches, a woman who needed someone to clean her house, asked my sister for help. Now my sister was already busy working every day, so she recommended me to the lady.

I began working that week and soon others called for me. Now I have work Monday through Saturday morning. I work half days, every other week, for 19 families.

I do have one big problem – I don't have a "green card," so I am not here legally. Mr. Smith, a local lawyer who helps people become legal, says I will have to find work in some area that is classified as "essential" in order to get a card. I worry about this all the time.

I go one evening every week to the First Baptist Church for English lessons. But it is hard to learn when everyone at my sister's house speaks Spanish. Very few businesses have workers who speak Spanish so shopping is hard.

This year my parents came to Nacogdoches. They found work immediately at the chicken processing plant – even got green cards. My youngest sister came with them and she goes to Nacogdoches High School. It is hard for her because she cannot speak English yet and few of the teachers can speak Spanish.

Now I have a special friend; I think he will ask me to marry him. I will say "yes" of course. We will be married in the Baptist Church for Spanish speakers. We go there every Sunday. When we marry, we will be able to rent a small mobile home in the area where my sister lives. It will be wonderful, wonderful, to have a place of my own!!!

Chapter VII
The Paschalls

OLD NAME, OLD FAMILY: THE PASCHALLS

Family histories offer fascinating views of the past as well as fine folk tales. In the community of my childhood, one of the oldest and best-known and best-represented families was the Paschall family. At one time, there were five Paschall women who had families in the community. Descendants enjoy sharing their great stories.

The Name

Paschall is a very old name. It first came into use when the children of Israel left Egypt under the leadership of Moses. The feasts which preceded the departure and, in later years commemorated it, were called "The Passover." The priest in charge of the celebration was referred to as Pashur. When the Greek language began to be used by the Jewish tradesmen, the form of the word was changed to the Greek "Pascha." From this came the English "Paschall" or the French "Pascal" or the Italian "Pasquale." When the festival came to be a part of the Christian tradition, it still retained the name Paschall, referring to Jesus as the Pascal

Lamb. Today we may hear such words as the Paschal candle, or Paschal day or Pascal feast in reference to services at Eastertime.

Originally, the name was used as a first name, then later as a surname. In 817, there was a Pope named Paschal I. Later, Paschall II was pope from 1099-1118 and Paschall III was elected antipope in opposition to Alexander III in 1165.

Paschalls Then and Now, There and Here

Today, Texas Paschalls believe that those first ones (those who became Tennesseans, Kentuckians, and then Texans) were found in France where they were faithful to the Huguenot Religion. It was religious persecution that forced them to move to England. Direct knowledge of them comes via William Paschall, a maker of pewter, in Bristol, England in early 1600. The record of the baptism of his son (the soon to become American) is found in the famous church: St. Mary, Red Cliff. The baptism of young Thomas Paschall was in October, 1634.

Like his father, Thomas grew up to become a successful maker of pewter, and when William Penn, a man in their church, began selling land in the "new world" the Thomas Paschalls bought 500 acres in what became known as Pennsylvania. Thomas brought his family and several servants from the English town of Bristol. Here are excerpts from the letter he wrote to his friend in England describing what they found and how they began their life in America. (In England the letter - shown here with spelling used by Mr. Paschall was printed in multiple copies and used to promote the portion of the new world that the Penns were selling.)

"My kind love remembered unto Thee and thy wife, and to all the rest of thy family, hoping that you are all in good health, as through the goodness of God we all are at the present writing excepting one of my servants, who was a carpenter and a stout young man ....the country is full of goods, brass and pewter lieth upon hand, that which sells best is linen cloath, trading cloath for the Indians. I brought Kersey and it doth not sell, broad cloath is wanted, and Perniston and iron pots. The Swedes use but little iron in building, for they will build and hardly use any other toole but an ax. ...Let all people know that have a mind to come hither to provide comfortable things for their passage, and also some provisions to serve them here, for although things are to be had at reasonable rates, it is so far to fetch. It is best to come provided for half a year....I have hired a house for my family for the winter and have gotten a little house on my land for my servants who live up- river.... Most of the settlers are ingenious; they plant but little Indian corne, nor tobacco. The people generally eat rye bread, but there is good wheat here. I have bought good beef, porke, and mutton at two pence per

pound, also turkeys, wild geese, curlews, pidgons, and pheasants. I have venison from the Indians very cheap. We had bears flesh this fall for little to nothing. There have been many horses sold of late to Barbadoes and here is plenty of rum, sugar, ginger, and molasses. ...Here are gardens of all sorts – peaches are in abundance as are apples, pears, plums, and quences. ...The Indians are quiet and peaceable, but when abused will seek revenge. ....William Penn is settling people in towns. ...There is good land, full of trees...the winter is sharp and the cattel are hard to keep. The people who come must work and attend to country affairs; they must be provided with some provision for some time in the country, and also have some to help along on board the whip.

Thomas Paschall
Pennsilvania, the last of January, 1683

Thomas and his wife, Joanna Sloper, had a son Thomas, who had a son John. It was John and his family who moved from Pennsylvania to North Carolina, Granville County. He and several of his boys served in the Revolutionary Army. In the next generation, there was William and next Alexander. Alexander is the one who homesteaded land in Weakley, Tennessee. He had been persuaded to move into the newly developing land of Tennessee and Kentucky by the group that went "west" with Daniel Boone. He is the Paschall from whom many of the East Texas and Northwest Texas Paschalls descend.

One evening, after a long, hard day of walking and looking at beautiful countryside, Alexander was tired and very thirsty. He spotted a place that seemed to lead to a spring, so he followed it, and there he came upon a quiet place with clear running water. He quietly walked a few steps toward the spring and suddenly he looked up to see a big black bear drinking from the spring. He stood in wonder, thinking it was one of the most beautiful sights he had ever seen. He watched until the bear moved on. Then Alexander drank his fill and he, too, moved on. After a good night's rest he made haste to complete the work necessary to homestead the land where he saw the "bear at the spring."

Many of Alexander's descendants in East Texas and in North West Texas are descended from Alexander through his son, Jesse Morgan Paschall or through his daughter, Nancy Paschall Pointer.

THE BEAR AT THE SPRING

The Place

Often descendants ask family members still living in Fulton, Kentucky or Weakley, Tennessee about the place of the bear and the first homestead. If they are lucky they are treated to a visit to the very place where the bear, and the Paschalls, found a home.

In the quiet of an early morning with the dew still on the grounds, one goes softly into the woods surrounding the stream of spring water. Only the early morning sounds of the birds disturb the quiet of the place. Even in the heat of summer, it is cool in the shade of these trees that grow close up to the stream of water. It is so still and quiet and beautiful that the visitor thinks she has reached a holy place.

A few yards away – up onto a higher plain of pasture land, one finds a small cemetery with Paschall names scattered among those buried long ago.

Still further along is the site of the original Paschall home, only in recent years gone to a non-Paschall family.

The town that borders Weakley, Tennessee is Fulton, Kentucky, and it was in Fulton that Alexander's sons grew up, went away to college, and eventually set up their medical practice. In those early days, physicians often made more money from selling medications than from seeing patients. Because of that, Dr. Gideon Paschall and Dr. N. J. Paschall soon had a fine building erected on the square for their pharmacy. They were proud to see their name above the fine new place: PASCHALL PHARMACY. And as time when by, it helped them reach their goal of financial security.

Patman Paschall

Patman Paschall, third son of Jesse Morgan Paschall, is the colorful subject of several Paschall folktales. Unlike Gideon and N. J., their brother, Patman, knew that medicine was not for him. In fact, since, as a young boy, when he had read stories about the wild land of Texas, he had yearned for the life of a Texas cattleman. He wanted more land, and more space than his part of the family property land in Kentucky provided.

He had married early and he and his wife, Rebecca, soon had a large family. There was Ben, Jessie, Perry, Rebecca, Catherine, Lucinda, and Newton. With the birth of the eighth one, Rebecca and the baby both died. With that tragedy Patman decided to leave Kentucky and start over in Texas, the place where he had always wanted to be. He moved to northeast Texas (today's Denton area) and began a successful trade in the cattle business.

By this time, the Civil War was in full swing, although Patman was still making cattle drives from Texas to Kansas. It is from that time period that we have the story called: "A Lesson in Putting Out the Wash." Here it is:

One day Patman had taken a drove of cattle to market and was going home alone. As he passed a farm house he noticed a woman standing in her yard, looking at a pile of clothes and crying in obvious frustration. Little children lingered around their mother tugging on her skirts.

Stopping his horse, Patman said, "Mam, I can see you have trouble here? Is there any way I can be of help?"

She replied, "My husband has gone to the war; my slaves have all run away; there is no one here except my children and me; all out clothes are dirty; and I don't know what to do."

"Well, I can show you how to wash clothes," he assured her, "I'm a widower with seven children, and I know something about putting out a wash!"

He began by making a fire around the wash pot, then filling the tubs with water, the work began, and eventually they had the mountain of clothes hanging on the lines to dry. Patman when on his way home!

Patman was fairly successful in business, but he had a terrible time keeping a wife. Soon after he moved to Texas he married a woman named Joanna. Now while she was able to care for the children when Patman volunteered for service in the Civil War, she soon contracted pneumonia and died before Patman could get home. With the large, growing family, Patman was released from military service and returned to their Texas home to care for the growing children!

But again, he felt the need of a wife and care-giver for the children. He began a search and soon he met a young widow with one child. She was a pretty lady, named Charity Long Berry. He called her, "Chattie," and it was a love match at first sight. Their first child was name Ada (descendants who talk of family history say, "Ader was born right about the breakup of the war between the states!) In due time Ada was joined by brothers and sisters: Bud, Lynn, Nannie, Lola Montez, Charlie, Cecil and Emma.

After the Civil War ended, Patman and Chattie decided he was too old to continue the long, demanding cattle drives. They thought he might be more suited to cotton farming. Now, Chattie was related to the Long Family in East Texas and she contacted them about the possibility of buying some of the good cotton land there. The contact put them in touch with a man who wanted to try cattle ranching. After correspondence by mail and telephone, the two men traded farms, "sight unseen."

It took several wagons to move the family from North-west Texas to East Texas. Some of the older boys helped with the move, although all the first set of children were adults with homes of their own. By the time the wagons reached Dallas, Chattie and baby Emma were sick, so Patman put them and the other girls on a train to Cumby. They stayed in a hotel there until the wagons came and picked them up to make the last leg of the move to their new cotton farm in Hopkins County.

A few years after the move, Chattie died. By that time the older girls had married and they took the younger children into their homes until they were grown.

Patman was a Master Mason, a well-read man, keeping up with world affairs by reading the Dallas Weekly Herald which was sent to him by rail to the Emory, Texas office. He ordered his favorite tobacco from Little Rock, Arkansas and it, too, came by rail. At times he had owned land in Kentucky, and in several places in Texas.

He was a strong father, but kind and considerate of all the children. He always brought gifts for the children when he returned from trips. Often he brought a large bag of nuts. He would say to the children, "Take a dose of this mineral oil then eat as many as you want."

A few months after Chattie died, Patman visited his brothers and their families in Fulton, Kentucky. Here's a tale the folks tell about that visit.

During the visit, Patman stayed with his brother N. J., a physician and owner of the local pharmacy. The N. J. Paschalls had a large, fine house near the center of town, and there they hosted a formal dinner to honor Patman and his visit. Now Patman had been a rough cattleman for some years and had adopted casual Texas manners. He was undoubtedly put-off by all the formality, for at the dinner table this is what happened. Toward the end of the long, extended meal, the lady to Patman's right, turned to him and asked, "Mr. Patman, tell me about your family; and (with awe in her voice) how many children do you have?" For some reason the question irritated Patman, and his sharp reply was, "Sixteen - legitimate ones, that is!" Oh my, the brothers said the lady almost swooned, and there were few questions for Patman during the remainder of the meal.

Patman soon returned to Texas and before long he married a local widow named Lou Morgan. She also preceded him in death. Eventually he moved to his youngest daughter's large home right in the center of the community and there, at age 80, he died. Stories that tell of his life are almost endless!

Today a few Paschall items can be spotted in descendants' homes. Among them are a dresser from Patman's bedroom, an large, iron bean pot used on the cattle drives and the large wedding portraits of Chattie and Patman, made by an artist toward the end of the Civil War and now hanging in the home of a Great-great grandson.

A CIVIL WAR WEDDING

When the subject of weddings surfaces among a gathering of Paschall women, someone always retells the story of the wedding of Newt and Sarah Jane Paschall. It happened long ago; in fact, it was during the Civil War, and we have the story today because a few years after the war, the Fulton newspaper asked Newt to retell the story for the local readers. Here are excerpts from that long-ago article. We Paschalls love to retell it - it may be our very favorite folk-tale!

Newt said that he had met Sarah Jane when she came to live with her aunts and the two of them had an understanding before he left home for the war. They had even set the date.

Unfortunately when the date came, there were Yankee soldiers all over town and getting Sarah Jane out was a major problem. But getting a marriage was an even greater problem. , Newt explained, "When we decided on the town where we could safely buy the certificate, I detailed twelve of my bravest men - all well-mounted, to go with me through the enemy lines and get the license. Along the way to the county office we met a fellow we knew, and fearing he would report us, we took him prisoner. When we got to the second town, I assigned two men on picket duty on each road into town.

At the county clerk's office, the little clerk asked my age; then he asked Sarah Jane's age. I did not know her exact age, so I turned to my faithful escort and asked, "Bob, how old is Sarah Jane?

Bob was a big tall man and he straightened himself up and looking as ancient as he could, he said, "I don't know but she's older than me."

The clerk said "I'll put down thirty!"

I paid in two dollar greenbacks and we left. As we swung into our saddles, we saw people standing all around. I apologized to them saying I regretted inconveniencing them but that in a short time we would be away. "Or," I said, "Should any of you wish to take a drink with a living wild Rebel you may do so at my expense."

It did seem that there was not a teetotaler in the town for they all but the clerk, rushed over for a drink. I asked the bartender how much

I owed him. He suggested a reasonable sum and I paid him in more greenbacks. I even bought a jug of whiskey for my boys. We left town with everybody happily.

By the next day, our spies reported that the Yankees had searched several houses in town looking for Sarah Jane. (Later Sarah Jane said she had made up he remind to get married and the whole Yankee army cold not prevent it. We planned for her to join us at our hideout on the following Saturday.)

Late, on that Saturday we reassembled in a dense forest bottom far from town. Along about mid-night I took Bob and we got Sarah Jane out of the boarding house with no problems.

Back at the camp, the new day dawned as bright and lovely as ever shown since Adam and Eve, and after a good breakfast of ham and eggs and tea and coffee, we were ready for our wedding. I dressed in a military suit that one of my men had got through enemy lines. It had well-polished brass buttons, and with my broad-brimmed hat, my boots and two six-shooters on my belt, I was ready. I even had a clean white shirt.

When the men and I rode to the place where we were to meet Sarah Jane, we found her dressed in a rustling silk gown, and tanks to a kind Providence, we did not encounter any trouble getting the brave young minister to the wedding site. During the ceremony, each soldier held his hat over his heart.

Out next task was to get Sarah Jayne home and get my men to safety. Fortunately I was able to get a little old man who had a mule and a dilapidated buggy to help me. In a few days, Sarah Jayne dressed in work clothes and she and the old man reached safety without incident. My men and I were soon safely back at Col. Crossland's headquarters. (We had earlier released our captive.)

Finally we were all safe, but it was a strange beginning for us!"

THOSE PECULIAR PASCHALLS

Little drops of water, little grains of sand, make the mighty ocean and the pleasant land. ...
Julia Fletcher

Despite the long and illustrious history of the Paschalls from Passover time until current times, there were those who were known by local folk as "Those Peculiar Paschalls." For example, in the time of our parents, there was Cousin Julian. If the time of his life were today, folks might say that he had "obsessive compulsive disorder," (OCD) that is, a high need for order in his life, but in his day, neighbors just said he was "peculiar." A present Paschall family historian, Mr. Joe Follis Bennett of Fulton, Kentucky, described him this way, "Julian was very, very, very methodical!" Mr. Bennett and Mr. Jerry Paschall shared these folk tales about methodical Paschalls .

Julian Paschall and his brother owned the only pharmacy in town – inherited of course from their father who was a local physician. Julian lived alone in the upper level of the old family home. His brother, Ed, lived alone in the lower level and while they occasionally talked together they often communicated via written notes.

Julian was in the pharmacy every day, opening it, filling prescriptions, and closing it. He never missed a day of work. Each day he walked to work, but at the end of the day he called his brother to come and drive him home. Brother Ed came when called, but rather than join him in the front seat, Julian choose to ride in the back seat.

Julian walked the same route to work each day and along the way he smoked a cigarette, striking the match to light it on a specific fence post. One year, the town changed the fencing, and in so doing, moved the post. With the post gone, Julian gave up smoking. He never smoked another cigarette!

On Fridays, he changed his routine by going from the pharmacy directly to the main restaurant in town. There he always sat at the same table; if someone else were at "his" table he asked them to move (they always complied with his request!). He never asked anyone to sit with him – he always ate alone! First, he ordered six bottles of beer. When he finished those (and he looked often at his watch to assure that his timing was perfect), he went to the bathroom, then, returning to his table, he ordered a cheese sandwich, one made with a special cheese that the restaurant owner ordered just for him. Finally he ordered another six bottles of beer, drinking them methodically so that he finished at the same time each evening. One day as he went to the bathroom, he realized that he had miscounted the beer bottles and had drunk on five. He recovered the 6th undrunk beer and took it to the bathroom with him so that he would not get off his regular time frame. Another day, after placing his order, the manager came to his table and said, "Mr. Paschall, we have only six bottles of the brand of beer that you like; will you consider another brand?"

"Certainly not," Julian replied; "and if you can't fill my order for the final six; I won't pay for the first six either!" (The poor restaurant owner then went down the street to another restaurant where he got the specified brand, and Julian was once again on tract!) Julian watched his watch carefully so that he began and ended his drinking at exactly the same time each Friday. Along with his dinner, Julian asked for a glass of water AND, HE ALWAYS EMPHASIZED that IT MUST HAVE FOUR (ONLY FOUR) CUBES OF ICE IN THE GLASS!

At home, Julian's evening routine included dressing for bed, taking six raw eggs and getting in bed to eat them. He threw the shells on the floor – three on one side and three on the other, knowing that the maid would pick them up the next morning.

On Sundays Julian ate both dinner and supper with his sister and her family. However, if cold slaw were on the menu, he excused himself and went back to his home to eat. Similarly, if the table settings included spoons at each place setting, he would say, Mary Helen, you know I do not use spoons – take these away. All this "to do" over not wanting a spoon even though he drank very sweet tea – just poured it into his glass but did not stir it". ("Good gracious!!!," said a fellow diner with disgust.)

Julian seldom went out of town, but one year a relative of his had an extra ticket for a performance in Chicago by Houdini and he invited Julian to go with him. They traveled by train and about half way along, Julian jumped up from his seat and yelled, "Hold your purses and bill folds – this man (he pointed to a man in uniform sitting in the row behind them) looks just like the picture of the thief in a post office picture we have in Fulton!"

Unfortunately, Julian had mistaken a train conductors' uniform for that of a prisoner! But he was not deterred. About half way through the program in Chicago he stood and walking out of the auditorium he said in a loud voice, "All of you people are crazy to watch something like this!" Apparently that was the last time anyone invited Julian to travel with them!

Julian lived methodically and he planned to die in the same way. As a friend of the local mortician, he was confident his will would be carried out. First, he went to the mortuary and lay down in several different coffins to assure that he would choose a comfortable one. Next he gave strict instructions that he would be dressed in pajamas and a robe – not a suit – and that his body would be turned on its left side!

Julian was not without good points. For example, he was known in Fulton for developing a special headache power that he claimed was a sure cure. Every Sunday he distributed (free of charge) packets of the powder to folks all over town. People did occasionally remind each other, after they had laughed together about his peculiar habits, that with his sharp mind and careful attention to detail, there was always accurate filling of all medical prescriptions as long as Julian worked at the pharmacy.

Julian died from a kidney disease in 1937 and his funeral was held in the Fulton home of one of his sisters. His wishes about dress and casket were carried out and the minister spoke of his high intelligence – "such a smart man," he said. They buried him in the large Paschall section of the Fulton cemetery, closing his service by singing, "When the Saints Go Marching In."

Others

Julian was not the only methodical one! The family endured these behaviors in others, as well. One of Dr. Jessie Paschall's grandchildren was a smart, well-educated woman (master's degree in accounting) who lived until recent years. She was an artist who lived in many places until she found that Mexico was her favorite place and thereafter she made it her home. They called her, Tippi. People said she was "one of a kind – a free spirit." For example, at her mother's funeral, the minister spoke at length, and at one point, the daughter rose from her pew and said in a loud voice, "Mother, I don't know where you are, but I certainly don't like what this preacher is saying!" As the congregation gasped with unbelief she sat down and the minister quickly finished his presentation.

After her mother's funeral, Tippi returned to her beloved Mexico where she lived and worked for the remainder of her life. At her death she was cremated and her ashes, at her request, were thrown to the winds in her chosen country.

Ad and Net

East Texans who are researching Paschall history find the story of the two old Paschall ladies (sisters) who returned, in their later years, to live in Fulton. The two moved into the house that had once been the grandest in the town – their Uncle N. J.'s homeplace. Now it was seriously deteriorated. It sat on the state line and one of the sisters claimed she lived in Kentucky and the other claimed to be in Tennessee. If they became angry with one another, they retreated to their on state (still in the same house, of course.) A young relative described it as "scarier than the house in the film, Psycho!"

Local historians and people, who just enjoy a folktale or two, tell of a time when a history student came to interview the two about their lives. She went away with a great story. "We were born during the terrible times of the War of Northern Aggression," Ad said. Net interjected, "our ancestors were among the founding fathers of these two towns (Fulton, Ky. and its adjoining torn of Weakly, Tenn.) With a sad sigh, Ad said, "It's a shame there have been no boys to carry on our prominent name (Paschall)."

Ad told about her community work in years past – active in the Prohibition movement and a member of Fulton's Women's Christian Temperance movement – editing its newsletter. We were always active in the Methodist Church, where Net taught the young men's Sunday School Class," they said.

Now they were lonely old ladies. Perhaps they drank a little too much, as some Paschalls did. Daily they sat at the windows overlooking the town, and each had their on bottle of Colonel Lee whiskey on their respective chairside tables. They sipped throughout the days.

The story goes that the ladies had goodly sums of money which they kept in the local bank. They were known, too, to have cultivated a strong friendship with the president of the bank. Occasionally, they would call him to come by for a glass of wine after work. Probably he felt some compassion for them but he also needed to protect their sizable accounts. With those thoughts in mind, he usually went to the old ladies' private parties when invited. However instead of wine, they served him a much stronger drink. Their strategy was to get him to drink enough to talk more freely than he would have done normally. They longed to know who among their friends and acquaintances had money in the bank. AND they tried to get him to share something about the size of those accounts. If they found that someone they knew had more money in the bank than they had, they immediately dropped their friendship!

As time passed, one of the old ladies died and word was passed through the community that the remaining one was a pitiful case. Of course the Methodist preacher went at once to console her. As they began to talk, she said, "Oh-h-h-h-, Pastor, woe is me. I lost my husband; I lost my child; I've lost most of my friends; and now I have lost my sister. Oh, oh!"

He responded, "Now Sister Paschall; you must surely know that we can rely on the Lord in times like these."

Not to be consoled, she sat up straight in her chair and said in a firm voice, "Pastor, I have broken with the Lord!" (Hearing that story, several old-timers in Fulton said, "Sounds just like a Paschall!).

Confessions of a Paschall

Today's Paschall historian, Mr. Joe Follis Bennett, says that he may be placed by many folks in this "Peculiar Paschall" bunch. In fact, he says, "I am very, very, very, methodical in everything I do." "And," he continued, "in some ways this is good and in some it is bad." He cites his daily routines of eating, sleeping, taking his medications, etc., at exactly the same time each day. He enjoys living alone and he prefers to go alone to whatever outside activity he is involved with on any day. For example, he times his arrival at church each Sunday morning just as services begin, but he sits on the back row and leaves just before the service is over to avoid needing to talk with others before the service or as they leave the church. Similarly he prefers to use drive-through restaurants so that he can pick up his food and take it home to eat rather than to go into the restaurant and sit among others for his meals.

He detests clutter in any form, keeping each of his possessions in a specific space. His regular in all his habits, eating at the same time each day, and (if possible) eating the same foods for each meal of the day.

He remembers that as a child he preferred sitting quietly with the adults, listening to them talk, rather than playing outdoors with the children. Similarly, he did not enjoy college nor the many social opportunities afforded a young man. His enjoyment of sports is vicarious, watching sports games on television in the privacy and quiet of his own home.

And, of course, he is not one to chat on the telephone.

As a pharmacist, he always chose to work in the back of the family pharmacy, where he dealt with medications, rather than to work in the front, serving people directly. Order is an important part of his life. Today, in retirement, Mr. Bennett continues to live a methodical lifestyle. For example, periodically he sets aside time to go through each room of his home and check items storied to assure that each is in its assigned place.

Others, too, fell into this category of "Peculiar Paschalls," but despite their penchant for order, which may appear excessive to outsiders, folks remember that any problems they may have caused have been overshadowed by the good they have done in their communities. Family and friends love to cite people like Dr. "Blue" Paschall, who is said to have successfully attended to the good health of whole town of Fulton for three generations. In Texas today, several prominent physicians are Paschall descendants. While few have been as prominent in national circles as Dr. John Norten Herbers (the White House Correspondent who wrote the book JUST SAY NO, MR PRESIDENT, during the Nixon administration), dozens have achieved success in medicine, agriculture, business, government, education, community and church leadership. Despite their enjoyment in discussing peculiar relatives, Paschall descendants take great pride in their family history. Through the years, family members and other folk have laughed together at these pecularities and pronounced them outside the norm, but at the same time they have loved each other and appreciated each's many contributions to family and community.

Today, Paschall descendants of the Tennessee/Kentucky Paschalls have moved further into Texas – from their early years in the northeast to northwest, south, the Panhandle and Deep East Texas. These many generations of Paschalls have blazed a wide trail – from Israel to France, on to England, then to Pennsylvania and next to North Carolina, then finally to Tennessee, Kentucky and Texas!

THE PASCHALL PENNY

This story began with the Civil War; i.e. with the great conflict between the northern and the southern states. At the time, the conflict and its ensuing war was called by several names such as the following ones which were used in various areas of the country.

War Between the States
War for Southern Independence
War of Rebellion
War of Aggression

When the war began, our family had yet to get to East Texas; however those in Kentucky suffered great trauma because there were family members on each side of the issue. Most joined the southern movement but there were others among them some who sided with the north.

The deadly war created great hardships across the nation and it was a foolish young man who went to war without serious fears of the dangers before him.

In Kentucky one of our kin decided he must fight for the south so he began getting ready to go. Of course his mother, his father, and others in the family had great fear for him. Now on the day that he was to leave, a neighbor came to visit – to say "good-bye." After they had visited for a while, he said, "N. J., I have to go; you will want some private time with your parents before you leave, but I have brought something for you to carry with you while you are away. And with that said, he reached into his pants pocket and brought out a brand new, shiny new. "Keep this," he said, "on your person all the time and when you sense it in your pocket, or perhaps chance to touch it as you reach for a handkerchief, remember that it's a sign that you will return home - to your family."

He continued, "Of course, if you have some special need and must spend it, that will be fine, too, but we hope you can keep it and that it will bring you back to us."

Believe it or not, the young soldier kept that penny through the entire war and when he came home, he said one evening, "Mama, you remember that penny Mr. Croft gave me before I went away. Well, I've got it safely home; please put it away until there's another war and another soldier."

After some discussion they decided to keep it in a safety deposit box at the Fulton bank. Today the Paschalls note that the "Paschall Penny" has seen several wars: the Spanish War in Cuba in 1898, WWI, WWII, and in recent times, the Korea war. But regardless who has the penny; it always comes home to a Paschall descendant. Today it is in Follis Bennett's keeping, with plans for it to go eventually to Dave Spurrier, a great, great, great, great nephew of N. J. Paschall. He is found among the Paschalls from N. J. Paschall to his daughter, Mary Flora Bennett, and thence to Joe Follis Bennett, then to Dave Spurrier and later to Michael Spurrier. Then on and on – a symbol of goodness and faith and love.

Today the Paschall Penny resides in a safety deposit box in Fulton, Kentucky.

Chapter VIII

Celebrating Christmas

EGGNOG BRANCH OR "CHRISTMAS, 1836"

In 1845, when classes began at Nacogdoches University, dramatic Texas history was just a few years past and it made for great class lectures and discussions. Here is one of the most fascinating tales told in those history classes.

It happened just two miles east of downtown Nacogdoches on Hwy 21 (the Old San Antonio Road) where there is a stream of water that the original Spanish settlers called El Canida de los Castanos or "the stream upon whose banks the chinquapin grows." Today the ever-flowing stream is known as "Egg Nog Branch." It got that name because of the celebration held on its banks at Christmastime in 1836. The branch was a favorite camping place for farmers coming and going to Nacogdoches to market. It was also the place where those who look upon the wine when it is red, stop to water their horses, dilute their alcohol, and take a drink all around.

When the news of Houston's splendid victory at San Jacinto reached the people of Nacogdoches there was general rejoicing and a great celebration was planned. On the 25th day of December, 1836, the celebration to honor the peace was held at the branch. It was a great day. Besides an abundance of wholesome provisions such as roast pig, fried chicken, fried squirrel, baked sweet potatoes, pinto beans, squash, and corn, there were cakes and pies galore.

All the pots and pans from local kitchens were pressed into service in the gigantic proportions of eggnog was made. Fifty dozen eggs were procured from all the farmers in the vicinity - milk and the necessary whiskey was also furnished, and an egg nog was created that had never before- or since - been seen. As has been told throughout the years, when the tables were cleared and left-overs were packed to take home, there was not a drop of egg nog remaining. Even so, nobody got drunk, everybody had a good time, and all went home rejoicing.

That was over a hundred and eighty years ago, but the branch still flow with water and it still bears the name it acquired at Christmas time in 1836: Eggnog Branch.

Thanks to Nayonna Millard and Virgie Scurlock for this tale.

A FAMILY CHRISTMAS STORY

When we were growing up, our family lived with our grandparents. We were there because our grandfather was a handicapped man who could no longer work the farm land, so, when Mother and Father married, they agreed to stay on in the family home and manage the farm.

Numerous aunts, uncles, and cousins lived nearby. We loved each other, but most of all, we loved our Grandfather dearly. He was a wise and compassionate man, much loved not only by his family, but by everyone in the community. He taught the Adult Sunday School Class from the time he was a young man until his death. Son of a Methodist Circuit Rider, I suppose he was as near to a Bible scholar as the community had.

One Christmas near the end of the Great Depression, when people were getting a little money, members of his Sunday School Class decided to buy him a new Bible for Christmas. His was worn by time and much use. Some of the pages were loose and the binding was torn and threadbare. The selection committee rode together into town to make the purchase. They bought a fine new Bible - the best one they could afford with the money they had collected. It had Jesus' words printed in red; it had colored maps of the Holy Land; and the cover was of fine leather. Its size was just right for carrying. The people took great pride in giving their teacher such a gift, and my Grandfather was delighted to get it.

On Monday morning after he had received the Bible on Sunday, one of the older men in the class came to our house for a visit with Grandfather. Of course the new Bible was the main topic.

"Is it all right?" The visitor asked.

"Oh yes, it's an excellent Bible, the finest I've ever seen," replied Grandfather.

But that was not enough assurance for the visitor. He continued,

"Now Bro. Johnson, are you sure the print is not too small?"

"Not atall; not atall!" exclaimed my grandfather in that old fashioned phrase used to emphasize a point: "Not atall!"

Years passed. Our beloved grandparents died, and in a few years our parents were gone as well. When we children distributed their belongings, my brothers gave Grandfather's Bible to me.

As I pondered this unselfish gift, I reasoned that it should go to the eldest grandson – one who would carry Grandfather's name. So that year, I determined to give it to my oldest brother for Christmas.

But first, it must be repaired. Like Grandfather's bible of old, it had loose pages, a torn cover, and many smudges from long years of much use.

Early in the fall, I took the bible to our local bookstore and ask that it be sent to a binder for repair and refitting with a new leather cover.

"Oh," exclaimed the manager, "that will be costly, and I can sell you a new one – a much better one – for half the cost."

"No," I replied, "I really want this one restored."

"But," the manager persisted, "the new one will be so much better."

I explained, "It is a family bible that holds great significance."

"Well," he suggested, "just take this old one and put it on a high shelf in your library and buy one of these nice new editions, one with a better concordance, one with a more current version!"

Again, I resisted buying the new one, and finally he agreed to send Grandfather's old Bible for new binding and a new cover. He figured the cost, and as I was about to pay him, he made one last effort.

Now, Mrs. Hallman," he said, "Look at this cost; are you really sure you want to pay this amount for an old Bible that will never look really new again; don't you think restoring this old and worn one is a poor decision?"

And I replied (in my grandfather's own words), "*Not atall; not atall*."

A COLD CHRISTMAS MADE WARM

It was a cold day in December, and on the icy streets of Chicago, a young boy struggled to sell all his papers. The north wind blowing over those cold great lakes cut through his clothes like giant saw blades.

Although there were shoppers about, few were interested in the morning paper. Thinking he must sell all of his papers if there was to be any Christmas money for his family, he decided to move from his regular sales post to stand just outside the large downtown department store. There its covered portico might give him a little warmth – at least he would be out of the wind.

As he moved wearily along, a fine mist began to fall, and even the protection of the store's portico was not enough to give any warmth in his wet clothes. And, of course, the longer he stood the colder he got.

Then a strange thing happened – a lady – well-dressed with furs and hat and muffs, stopped to buy a paper. After she gave him a coin and took the last paper she looked at him carefully, and then said, "Please come into the store with me." Puzzled, he followed close behind her less he be thrown out. She led him directly to the boys department. When a salesman approached she said, "We need dry clothes from the underwear out, a heavy coat, a cap, and boots with wool socks."

"Have a seat." the man said to the boy, "and I will show you what we have."

Soon the lady had selected an entire wardrobe for the wet, cold, and confused boy.

The little fellow was speechless as the man showed him into a changing room and quickly brought to him the dry and warm clothing. When he had changed all his clothes and was seated to try on the boots and socks, the woman, who had stood by, said to the clerk, "Please put all this on my bill, and when you have him fitted with the boots be sure to give him a bag to carry his wet things home in."

She turned to leave, and suddenly the speechless boy called out to her: "Mam, mam," he cried, "Who are you?"

"Are you Christ's wife?!"

Given to Patsy Hallman by Willie Lee Campbell Glass

THE YEAR SANTA CLAUS CAME TWICE

It was in the dead of winter in 1890, and Great-Grandfather and Great-Grandmother Tatom, with their seven children and the new baby, had just moved to a different farm to continue their lives as share-croppers. The move was made in just a few wagon trips – one for their farming tools – plows, hoes, rakes, etc., and one for the house plunder – and one for the beds, chairs, dressers, dining table, kitchen cabinet, and the wood cook stove. The third trip brought Ma and the younger of the children, along with their clothing and other bits and pieces such as coal oil lamps, the sewing machine, quilting frames and similar items.

They got the four-room house all set up in time for Christmas – front room where Ma and Pa and the baby slept, the girls room, boys room, and the kitchen. Of course there was a back porch where much work took place and the front porch where folks sat to relax on spring, summer, and fall evenings. It was by far the best house they had ever lived in and they had been in several because Pa liked to change farms about every two years – always looking for better farm land or a better house.

In the days following the move, Pa cut wood for their own fireplace and cook stove and also for sale in order to have cash money for the winter. On Christmas Eve he loaded all the wood he could spare and set out for town to sell the wood and buy their "Christmas." Parking on the hitch lot in Sulphur Springs, he sold out in record time; then he set about making his purchases: first were the gifts for the children's Christmas stockings. He bought a pocket knife for each boy and a small doll for each girl. On to the grocery store he bought the items Ma sent for – a box of "sode," a sack of sugar, 25 pounds of flour, and seven big pieces of hard candy. Finally, he bought an apple and orange for each child.

It was long after dark when Pa drove in home. Ma had already fed the children and put them to bed. She had his supper warm in the oven and after he ate, they filled the stockings. How pretty the stockings looked all hung on the mantle. As they stood back admiring them, a horrified look came on Ma's face. "What's wrong," Pa asked. And with unbelievable wonder, Ma replied, "We forgot the baby! And I can't think of a thing in the house that we could put out for him." Pa couldn't think of anything either, so they just went to bed, hoping an idea would come to them in the night.

And it did. Next morning, the children got up and shared the delights of all children everywhere as they emptied their Christmas stockings. Santa had, once again, been good to them. As they rejoiced over their gifts, Ma said, "Look. Here's a note on the mantle from Santa. Let's see what it says."

Dear Children. I did not know that you have a new baby until I got here. I'll come back tomorrow night to bring his gift.
Love. Santa Claus

Soon after breakfast, Pa told the children he had to go back to town with some wood that some families needed. He loaded all his wood (except for the needs of the day) on the wagon and set out for town. Going from house to house, he soon sold it. Then he found an open store and made his purchases. Driving along at a fast clip, he was home for a late Christmas dinner.

That night the children hung Baby Arthur's stocking. And, sure enough! Santa Claus was true to his word, for the next morning the stocking was filled with a soft, cuddly Teddy Bear. And laid along the mantle was another big piece of hard candy for each of the children!

Oh, it was a good time – the year Santa Claus came twice!

"CHRISTMAS IS COMING, CHRISTMAS IS COMING!"

It was 1943, and the whole world, including people on remote farms in Northeast Texas, were heavily immersed in World War II. All the young men had left the farms to join the military forces; most of the young women had moved to the cities to work in the munitions factories; and gasoline, shoes, sugar and all sorts of necessities were rationed.

Nevertheless, Christmas was coming, and in every home preparation must be made.

My ingenious Mother began early, for there was much to be done. For example, she must make most of the items Santa would bring – doll clothes, pop guns, wooden toy cars, sweaters and new pajamas. She worked with her coping saw, with discarded wooden apple crates, with rubber from old enter tubes and with fabric from colorful feed sacks. She was clever in use of these materials to replace rubber and metal and other items no longer available because of the war needs. With her sewing machine going top speed during the hours we were at school on days between Thanksgiving and Christmas, Santa's bag was gradually filled.

As far as the Christmas dinner was concerned, she and my grandmother were fairly comfortable about the food for the large family gathering. With chickens and eggs, hams, and garden stuff, there would be little problem in producing a feast.

But how would they get the ingredients for the Christmas candy? There was almost no sugar to be had, and certainly the stores wouldn't have the nuts traditionally used for candy making. Our farm had no nut trees. What could to be done?

The families – and the guests who would come to our house during the season – expect platters of divinity, fudge, peanut brittle, and Martha Washington bonbons. Of course, women in every household were packing boxes of goodies to send to their soldiers – Regardless of the costs in money and effort; our fighting men must have Christmas candies from home? "Oh, my," the women exclaimed, "what can we do?

And this is what they did in our household - for after all, Christmas was coming! My mother wrote a postcard to her father, asking him to bring a bushel of hickory nuts from his farm when he and Grandmother Smith came for Thanksgiving. Our father carried a water bucket with him on his next squirrel-hunting foray and returned with it full of black walnuts from trees deep in the woods. These, with the peanuts from a neighbor's farm, would be adequate for the nuts, but what about the sugar?

My father took on that problem. You see he knew a man or two who often sold their family's ration coupons when they needed cash more than they needed sugar and shoes. Father organized a collection – of sugar – and of money to convert to sugar coupons. With those resources, and plenty of the locally made ribbon cane syrup and the sometimes-available white syrup, the ladies were finally ready to make the precious Christmas candy.

A day was set to produce the goodies; our aunts came to help and they with my mother and grandmother began. Actually, they had been working for a couple of weeks on getting the nuts ready. The black walnuts and hickory nuts had been set in the sun to dry, then hulled, and finally cracked with a heavy hammer pounding them on a big rock that sat near the smokehouse where nuts were stored. Pecans were opened with a smaller hammer that carefully cracked them on a wooden block. Then, on cold winter evenings, the family sat around the fireplace and picked out the nuts. These, they carefully saved until the candy-making day.

Soon after breakfast they began. I can see the scene, even now, in my mind's eye. Granted it was from a child's perspective, but it was a special day and many of the scenes were frozen in time for delightful Christmas memories. Grandmother Johnson sat in her favorite kitchen chair that was placed by the wood box. Her main job was beating the great bowls of eggs whites for the divinity – of course; she used a flat wisk for this time-consuming job. Mother mixed together ribbon cane syrup and peanuts and set them on the back of the wood cook stove to cook ever so slowly all morning. Others kept a close watch on the mixture for the divinity. We children played about the kitchen, hoping for samples.

When all the candies were cooked and cooled, they were stored in shoe boxes lined with wax paper. Heavier boxes, salvaged from the general store that stood in the center of our community, were packed to send afar. After much trial and error they learned that the best method was to wrap each candy piece in butter paper (used normally for wrapping the pounds of butter sold at the local store) then placed between layers of cotton in small syrup buckets and the buckets set tightly into a heavy box. With these methods they were confident the candies would still be edible when they reached our soldiers. These soldiers were sons of our neighbors – some with three and four boys from a single family. Then, of course, there was Mother's brother, our Uncle Howard in the Pacific on Nimitz' staff, and there were boys in Europe and Africa who had once been in Mother's first grade classes. From our small community alone there were 66 soldiers – scattered all over the world!

Then Christmas came, and it was a great and holy time for us all!

CHRISTMAS COMES TO EVERYONE

When God revealed himself to humankind,
His messages of love, and joy,

Of forgiveness, guidance, and life eternal,
Came not to a few chosen people, But rather to everyone.

He came to an inn-keeper,
Who found an alternative way to help a young family in need.

He came to shepherds – night workers – low-paid hired hands,
With no status at all, simple folk who responded with wonder and belief.

He came to wise men, scholars who could read the stars,
Those knowledgeable men, guided by sages of old, believed in God's promises.

He came to a young husband, bewildered, perplexed, committed and caring,
A man of faith, willing to assume the responsibilities that became his lot.

He came to a young woman, innocent afraid, faithful.
She who "pondered all these things and kept them in her heart."

He came to an old man, who was in the Temple to worship
And while he was there, he encountered God's own son!

He came to a woman who volunteered at the Tenple,
She was surprised by joy when she saw the promised Messiah.

For in this gift of Jesus, we see God,
With his love, his forgiveness, and his compassion.

He comes to you and me and all who accept this holy gift!
No wonder we celebrate! Goodness incarnate.

Patsy J. Hallman

About the Author

Dr. Patsy Johnson Hallman grew up in Miller Grove, Texas. She attended East Texas State Teachers' College in Commerce, graduated with honors and began teaching in El Paso, Texas, in 1955. Eventually, she relocated in Nacogdoches, Texas, where she taught high school as she pursued her master's degree in education at Stephen F. Austin State University.

By 1969, Dr. Hallman was part of the SFA faculty, teaching home economics. In 1970, she published her first work, "Role Modeling for the Student Teacher" in the Texas Teacher Education Forum. By 1973, she had earned her doctorate in management from Texas Women's' University.

Dr. Hallman has earned a variety awards as well, named SFA's Distinguished Professor in 1990, the American Association of University Women's Woman of the Year in 1993, and she was inducted into the Nacogdoches Women's Hall of Fame in 2003.

In addition, Dr. Hallman was instrumental in facilitating SFA's strong field-based teacher education research and served as the Associate Dean of Education for eight years, as Dean for three years. After approximately 60 published academic and non-fiction works and 36 years of service to SFA, she retired in 2005.

Since retirement, most of Dr. Hallman's volunteer time has been devoted to the Nacogdoches' Old University Building where she has researched and promoted this historical treasure, a unique feature of the rich tapestry of Nacogdoches' heritage. In spite of Dr. Hallman's lengthy list of folklore and historical publications, she claims she does not consider herself a writer, but a story teller. She currently resides in Nacogdoches with her husband, Dr. Leon Hallman. Her children are Dave Spurrier and Bethany Spurrier.

(Excerpted from the *The Daily Sentinel.*)

www.ingramcontent.com/pod-product-compliance
Lightning Source LLC
Chambersburg PA
CBHW060525080526
44586CB00012B/618